Is It Burnout or Depression?

How to Tell Work Burnout, Clinical Depression, and Autistic Burnout Apart, and Know What to Do Next

Evie Dove Huynh

Decoding the Overlap, Book 4

The Decoding the Overlap Series: for the questions that come before the diagnosis.

This book is for general educational and informational purposes. It does not provide a diagnosis, psychotherapy, medical advice, or an individualized treatment plan, and no particular outcome is promised.

Persistent exhaustion, loss of function, major changes in mood or interest, and other symptoms discussed here can have mental and physical causes. Decisions about diagnosis, medication, testing, treatment, or urgent care should be made with an appropriately qualified health professional who can assess your circumstances.

If you are in immediate danger or think you may act on thoughts of suicide or self-harm, seek emergency help where you live. In the United States, you can call or text 988 for the 988 Suicide & Crisis Lifeline.

Names and personal details in illustrative scenarios are fictional composites created to explain patterns. They are not intended to depict or misrepresent any identifiable person.

ISBN: 978-1-911838-65-4

Table of Contents

Preface

Burnout and depression are often discussed as though they were two neat boxes with a clean line between them. Research does not support that level of certainty. The World Health Organization defines burnout in ICD-11 as an occupational phenomenon linked to chronic workplace stress that has not been successfully managed, not as a medical condition. Depression is a mental disorder that can affect mood, interest, sleep, concentration, energy, appetite, self-worth, and functioning across settings. Studies comparing burnout and depression find substantial overlap, while researchers still disagree about how separate the constructs are (World Health Organization, 2019; Bianchi et al., 2015; Koutsimani et al., 2019).

A third pattern complicates the picture for autistic adults. Autistic burnout has been described in peer-reviewed qualitative research as prolonged exhaustion accompanied by loss of skills or function and reduced tolerance for sensory or other demands. The research base is growing, including newer work on measurement, but it remains younger than the evidence base for depressive disorders (Raymaker et al., 2020; Mantzalas et al., 2022, 2024). That matters because a person can use the same everyday word, "burnout," for experiences that arise from different contexts and need different kinds of assessment and support.

The practical problem is not that people lack advice. They have too much advice, most of it written after the label has already been chosen. "Rest more" can be sensible when demands have exceeded capacity. "Get active" can be part of evidence-based treatment for depression. "Change jobs" can be reasonable when work is the main driver. None of those instructions is a reliable diagnostic test, and any of them can be poorly timed when applied to the wrong problem.

This book offers a structured way to think before acting. Its central tool, the Three Question Check, asks about context, capacity, and change. Where did the problem start and where is it strongest? What has changed in your ability, interest, and tolerance? What happens when demands, support, rest, or activity change? The answers are treated as clues, not verdicts. They help you build a timeline, notice patterns, and decide what information to take to a doctor or mental health professional.

This is Book 4 in the Decoding the Overlap series, which is written for the part of the process that comes before a settled diagnosis. The book is aimed mainly at working adults who are exhausted and uncertain about the next step. Partners, family members, managers, and clinicians may also find the distinctions useful, but the text speaks to the person trying to make sense of their own pattern.

No chapter can determine whether you have depression, autistic burnout, occupational burnout, or more than one at the same time. The book is educational, not a substitute for medical or mental health care, and it does not tell you to start, stop, or change medication. Its purpose is narrower and more useful: to help you ask a better question, collect better evidence from your own life, and carry that evidence into the right conversation.

Introduction: When Exhaustion Stops Explaining Itself

Maya had a decision to make by Friday.

Her manager had offered two weeks of leave after she cried in a meeting she had led without difficulty for years. A friend told her to take the leave, sleep, and come back with firmer boundaries. Her sister said the crying was the least important part. Maya had stopped caring about food, music, sex, messages, and a promotion she had chased for eighteen months. She was not only tired of work. She was tired in places where work could not reach her.

Then a third person complicated things. Maya's autistic cousin asked a different set of questions: Had fluorescent light become harder to tolerate? Was speech taking more effort? Did ordinary errands feel like multi-step exams? Was she recovering when she was left completely free of demands, or merely becoming more withdrawn?

Three conversations, three possible stories, one exhausted person.

This is the problem the book is built around. "Exhausted" describes a state. It does not tell you what produced it. "Can't focus" describes an impairment. It does not tell you whether the main driver is depression, chronic workplace stress, sensory overload, sleep deprivation, anemia, medication effects, a mix of factors, or something else. The more familiar the symptom, the easier it is to mistake recognition for explanation.

The Label Changes the Question

A useful label should do more than make an experience sound familiar. It should narrow the questions worth asking. Work burnout directs attention toward chronic job stress, the relationship between a person and a job, and whether symptoms are especially tied to work.

Depression directs attention toward mood and loss of interest or pleasure, duration, severity, functioning across settings, safety, medical contributors, and evidence-based treatment. Autistic burnout directs attention toward cumulative demands, masking, sensory and social load, loss of skills or function, and whether the person's available capacity has fallen below the demands placed on it (World Health Organization, 2019, 2025; Raymaker et al., 2020).

Those directions overlap. A hostile job can contribute to depression. Depression can make a manageable job feel impossible. An autistic person can have occupational burnout, autistic burnout, depression, or combinations of them. A holiday may reveal useful information, but improvement or non-improvement over a week does not settle a diagnosis.

That is why this book refuses the popular shortcut that says burnout improves with rest while depression does not. Reality is less tidy. Rest can help a depressed person who is sleep deprived. Structured activity can help depression, but that does not mean forcing an exhausted autistic person through escalating demands is therapeutic. A better approach is to look at the pattern as a whole.

The Three Question Check

The Three Question Check gives you three places to look.

The first is context: where did the problem begin, and where is it strongest? Occupational burnout is defined around the occupational setting. Depression can spread across work, home, relationships, hobbies, appetite, sleep, and self-evaluation. Autistic burnout may be linked to sustained cumulative demands that are not confined to paid employment (Raymaker et al., 2020; Mantzalas et al., 2022).

The second is capacity: what exactly has become hard? A person can still want to read a novel but be unable to process a page. Another person may be physically able to read and feel no pull toward anything that used to matter. Neither pattern proves a diagnosis, but the distinction between desire and usable capacity is worth recording.

The third is change: what shifts when conditions change? Does a low-demand weekend restore some function? Does interest return before energy? Does gentle activity create a little momentum, or does it reliably deepen an already severe capacity crash? Does reducing sensory load alter the day? These are observations, not experiments you must force yourself to complete.

Throughout the book, you will collect those observations into a clinician handoff: a short account of onset, context, function, mood, interest, sleep, appetite, physical symptoms, stressors, neurodivergent traits if relevant, medication changes, and safety concerns. You do not need medical vocabulary. You need a pattern that another person can examine.

What This Book Will Not Do

It will not give you a score that announces what you "really have." Screening questionnaires can be useful in clinical and research settings, but self-scoring a few overlapping symptoms cannot resolve a difficult differential. It will not tell you that one treatment is always right for one label. It will not turn autistic burnout, a developing research concept, into a settled medical diagnosis.

It will also not make work the villain by default. Some people need a different job. Some need treatment for depression. Some need both. Some need medical evaluation for a physical cause of fatigue. A book that begins with a predetermined answer is not much help to a reader whose problem is uncertainty.

What follows is a sequence. First we separate the terms. Then we examine the three questions. Then we deal with overlap, medical rule-outs, and next steps. By the end, the aim is not certainty produced by a book. It is a cleaner, more defensible account of what has been happening, what has changed, and who should help you decide what it means.

Chapter 1: Same Face, Different Stories

Daniel was good at naming other people's burnout and terrible at recognizing his own uncertainty. He worked in software, managed a small team, and had spent six months waking with the thought that he could not do another day. By Sunday afternoon he became irritable because Monday was coming. Meetings felt pointless. He had begun referring to projects he once liked as "the same theater with different slides."

Then his employer shut down for ten days over the holidays. Daniel expected to sleep for three days and feel like himself again. Instead, the first thing that returned was not energy but curiosity. He cooked because he wanted to, walked to a record shop, and spent an hour comparing old jazz pressings. On the sixth day he still felt tired, but his sense that everything was pointless had loosened.

That pattern did not prove burnout. It gave him information. The work connection was strong, some interest outside work was available, and a real reduction in job demand changed the picture. Had nothing outside work come back, or had hopelessness and loss of pleasure spread through the entire break, the questions worth asking would have shifted.

Chapter principle: Similar symptoms can carry different information depending on context, pattern, and time. The job is not to match yourself to a stereotype. It is to notice which features travel across settings, which stay tied to particular demands, and which changes deserve professional assessment.

Overlap Is the Starting Point

Fatigue, concentration problems, irritability, sleep disturbance, reduced motivation, withdrawal, and reduced performance can appear in several states. That shared surface is why internet checklists often feel persuasive. A list can tell you that something is wrong. It is much weaker at telling you why.

Research on burnout and depression reflects the same difficulty. A major review by Bianchi and colleagues identified extensive overlap and argued that the distinction is less clear than many popular explanations suggest. A later systematic review and meta-analysis by Koutsimani and colleagues found strong relationships but concluded that the evidence did not justify treating burnout and depression as identical constructs. The disagreement itself is useful. It warns us against pretending that one symptom, one weekend, or one quiz can settle the question (Bianchi et al., 2015; Koutsimani et al., 2019).

The safest reader-facing conclusion is modest: overlap is real, and context matters. If someone tells you, "Burnout is only exhaustion, depression is only sadness," they are simplifying both. If someone tells you, "They are exactly the same thing," they are stepping beyond what the evidence can settle.

A Symptom Has Geography

Imagine the same complaint in three places: "I can't focus."

At work, Priya reads the same email four times, loses the thread during meetings, and feels a jolt of dread when the notification sound goes off. At home she can follow a complicated recipe and spend an evening absorbed in a mystery novel. That pattern makes the occupational context worth examining.

Now change the scene. Priya cannot follow the work email, the recipe, the novel, or a conversation with her partner. Food tastes flat. Her favorite comedy does not seem funny. She feels guilty for being "useless" even when no one has criticized her. The symptom has spread. That broader pattern makes depression and medical causes more important to assess.

Change it again. Priya is autistic. During a long period of relocation, family conflict, social demands, and masking at work, she loses her ability to manage grocery stores, phone calls, unexpected changes, and speech under pressure. Quiet, familiar routines reduce the strain, but her previous level of function does not quickly return. That pattern raises a different set of questions about cumulative demand and autistic burnout, while still leaving room for depression or physical illness.

The same phrase, "I can't focus," has different geography.

Do Not Turn Clues Into Tests

Readers understandably want a decisive question. "Do I feel better on vacation?" sounds promising. So does "Am I sad?" or "Do I still care about my hobbies?" None is strong enough by itself.

A person with severe workplace stress can develop major depression. Someone with depression may feel temporarily better when a pressure is removed. An autistic person in burnout may also become depressed. Physical illness can sit underneath or beside any of these patterns. Good differential thinking is cumulative. You look for several pieces that point in a similar direction and for pieces that do not fit.

This is also why the title of this book asks a question rather than announcing a test. The aim is to improve the quality of the question until the next step becomes clearer.

The Cost of the Wrong Shortcut

The wrong shortcut does not always cause dramatic harm. Sometimes it simply wastes time.

Marcus spent almost a year treating every crash as a productivity problem. He downloaded focus apps, moved his wake time earlier, joined a five-a.m. accountability group, and treated each failed routine as proof that he lacked discipline. The important information was that his exhaustion had become whole-life, his appetite had changed, and he no longer enjoyed weekends he had once protected fiercely. The productivity tools did not address the question in front of him.

Another reader could make the opposite error. A person whose symptoms remain strongly job-linked may assume that nothing can change until a psychiatric treatment "fixes" them, while leaving an untenable work pattern untouched. The point is not that medication is wrong or job change is right. The point is that the explanation shapes what gets examined.

Start a Plain Timeline

You do not need a mood-tracking system with twenty variables. Begin with four anchors.

Write down roughly when the problem became noticeable. Mark what was happening at work, at home, and in your health around that time. Note the first function that changed, not only the first feeling. Then mark any period when the load changed enough to reveal a difference.

"September: new manager, two vacancies on team. October: started waking at four. November: stopped cooking after work. December: ten days off, reading interest returned on day five, energy still low."

That is more useful than "I have been burnt out forever." It is also more useful than trying to remember six months of fluctuating symptoms in a fifteen-minute appointment.

Three Stories Can Share One Symptom

Maya had stopped cooking after work. That sentence sounds almost useless until you ask what sits underneath it. For Maya, the problem started with a reorganization. She could still spend Saturday morning testing a new recipe and still looked forward to dinner with friends. What failed was the last hour of a workday. By then, deciding what to chop felt like one demand too many.

Daniel also stopped cooking. He did not want the food he used to like, whether it was Tuesday night or Sunday afternoon. When his sister offered to make his favorite meal, he felt guilty that he could not summon interest. The loss was not tied neatly to the office.

Priya stopped cooking too. She wanted familiar food, but after months of rising sensory strain the supermarket lights, package decisions, appliance noise, and cleanup had become difficult to tolerate. A meal delivery that removed five steps made eating much easier. The visible behavior was the same. The route to it was not.

This is why symptom counting reaches its limit quickly. Exhaustion, withdrawal, irritability, sleep change, concentration problems, and a drop in ordinary functioning can appear across more than one condition. Research comparing burnout and depression finds a meaningful association between them while also showing that the question of overlap is not settled by a single shared symptom (Bianchi et al., 2015; Koutsimani et al., 2019). Autistic burnout research adds another pattern in which chronic exhaustion can appear with loss of skills and increased sensory sensitivity (Raymaker et al., 2020).

The useful question is not, "Do I have this symptom?" It is, "What pattern does this symptom belong to?"

Look for Direction, Not Drama

People often wait for a dramatic sign because dramatic signs feel more trustworthy. They imagine that depression should look like being unable to get out of bed, that work burnout should end in a sudden collapse, or that autistic burnout should involve an unmistakable loss of speech or daily skills. Real presentations are often quieter. A person may continue working, parenting, paying bills, and answering messages while a pattern becomes steadily more expensive to maintain.

That makes direction more useful than drama. Is the problem narrowing toward work, or spreading across settings? Is pleasure absent, or merely inaccessible when demand is high? Are sensory and social tasks becoming harder in a way that is disproportionate to physical effort? Is there a new change in sleep, appetite, pain, breathlessness, medication, illness, or substance use that deserves medical attention?

None of those questions diagnoses the problem. Together, they make the next conversation less vague.

A good note therefore records change in plain language. "I am exhausted" is important but broad. "For eight weeks I have been exhausted by 3 p.m. on workdays, but I can still spend two hours gardening on Sunday and enjoy it" gives a clinician more structure. So does, "I am just as flat on annual leave as I am at work, and I have stopped wanting things I normally enjoy." So does, "I want to see people, but conversation and noise now cost so much that I avoid both."

Specificity is not about proving your theory. It is about making the pattern visible.

The First Decision Is About Safety and Scope

Before comparing labels, decide whether this is a self-observation problem or a get-help-now problem. Thoughts of suicide, a sense that you may not be able to keep yourself safe, severe inability to eat or drink, new confusion, major physical symptoms, or a sudden and marked change in functioning need timely professional assessment. In the United States, the 988 Suicide & Crisis Lifeline is available by call or text at 988, and immediate danger warrants emergency services (Substance Abuse and Mental Health Services Administration, 2025).

The next decision is scope. If a change is mild, recent, and clearly tied to a short period of unusual demand, recording it for a week or two may be reasonable. If it is persistent, worsening, affecting several parts of life, or accompanied by symptoms associated with depression, medical illness, or significant loss of function, the threshold for professional assessment should be lower.

This book repeatedly asks you to observe before you conclude. That is not indecision. It is the discipline of differential thinking.

Build a Baseline Before You Change Everything

There is a practical problem with making five changes at once: if you feel different afterward, you will not know why. Someone who simultaneously takes a week off, changes medication, stops caffeine, cancels all social plans, and moves back in with family has created a new life, not a useful observation.

When safety allows, build a short baseline first. Choose three ordinary markers you can describe without scoring your worth. For example, note how long it takes to start work, whether you can enjoy one familiar activity, and how much recovery a routine social interaction requires. Record sleep and appetite only as observations, not as grades. If you are autistic or suspect you may be, add a sensory marker such as tolerance for noise, light, travel, or unexpected conversation.

Then record meaningful changes in context. A deadline ended. A weekend had no obligations. You worked from home. You had a supportive visit. You reduced meetings. You began treatment. You were ill. These events help you see whether symptoms move with the environment, remain broadly present, or change unevenly.

The purpose is not to turn your life into a laboratory. It is to replace a blurred memory with a small amount of usable evidence.

Ask One Better Question Today

If you do nothing else after this chapter, complete one sentence:

"Something changed around ______, and since then the clearest difference has been ______."

Do not force a label into either blank. A strong answer might be, "Something changed around the promotion in March, and since then the clearest difference has been that work irritates me before I even open the laptop." Another might be, "Something changed around late winter, and since then the clearest difference has been that nothing feels worth starting, even when I have no obligations."

That sentence is not a diagnosis. It is a starting point with a date, a direction, and a visible change. That is far more useful than one more hour of arguing with yourself about whether your exhaustion is real enough to count.

In a Nutshell

The surface symptoms are not the diagnosis. Fatigue, poor concentration, irritability, withdrawal, and reduced performance can belong to more than one story.

The first move is to stop asking which label sounds most familiar and start asking where the symptoms live, what exactly has changed, and what happens when circumstances change. Those observations will not diagnose you, but they can expose patterns that a generic checklist misses.

Keep the timeline. We will use it again when we examine work burnout, depression, autistic burnout, and the Three Question Check in more detail.

Chapter 2: Work Burnout Has a Boundary

At 4:42 on a Wednesday afternoon, Elena closed a spreadsheet and felt something close to disgust. The numbers were ordinary. The client was not difficult. What bothered her was the thought of spending one more hour pretending the work deserved the urgency everyone attached to it.

At six, she met a friend to help paint a small bedroom. She expected to cancel. Instead, once she was holding a roller and arguing about whether the wall was gray or blue, some animation returned. She laughed. She stayed late. She was tired when she left, but the tiredness did not feel poisoned.

The next morning, the same spreadsheet produced the same recoil.

Elena's pattern does not establish a diagnosis. It illustrates a feature built into the World Health Organization's definition: burn-out in ICD-11 refers specifically to the occupational context. WHO describes it as resulting from chronic workplace stress that has not been successfully managed and characterizes it through exhaustion, increased mental distance or cynicism toward the job, and reduced professional efficacy (World Health Organization, 2019).

Chapter principle: When you use the term occupational burnout precisely, the job is not background scenery. It is part of the definition. The stronger and more specific the work link, the more useful it becomes to examine the conditions of the job instead of treating exhaustion as a free-floating personal failure.

Burnout Is Not a Medical Diagnosis

Popular language often stretches "burnout" to mean any state of depletion. WHO uses the term more narrowly. In ICD-11 it appears as an occupational phenomenon in a section concerning factors that influence health status or contact with health services, not as a disease or medical condition. WHO also says the term should not be applied to experiences in other areas of life (World Health Organization, 2019).

That does not make burnout trivial. A problem can be serious without being a disease. It means the label tells us what domain to inspect: the relationship between chronic workplace stress and the worker's experience.

This distinction also prevents a common category error. Parenting strain, caregiving overload, financial stress, and chronic sensory demand can all exhaust a person. Calling all of them occupational burnout removes the very boundary that makes the term useful.

The Three Parts Point Back to Work

The first dimension, exhaustion, is the easiest to recognize and the least specific. Many conditions produce exhaustion. The second, mental distance, negativity, or cynicism related to the job, adds occupational information. The third, reduced professional efficacy, concerns the sense of being less effective in the work role.

Taken together, those dimensions direct attention toward a pattern. Someone may dread the inbox, feel emotionally detached from customers, become cynical about goals that once mattered, and believe their work no longer makes a difference. The details vary by occupation, but the job remains central.

A nurse may become emotionally distant because every shift feels like triage without enough staff. A teacher may stop preparing imaginative lessons because each new initiative seems to disappear by term's end. A founder may feel contempt for a company they built because every week has become a rescue operation. Those are not diagnoses. They are occupational stories.

Ask What Happens Off the Clock

The phrase "off the clock" is imperfect for remote workers, carers who also have paid jobs, and people whose work messages follow them home. Still, it gives you a useful question: when work is genuinely absent, what remains?

Luis noticed that his Sunday mornings were often good until he opened his calendar. He could enjoy breakfast, talk with his daughter, and plan a bike ride. Then the first glance at Monday's schedule produced tension, fatigue, and an urge to lie down. This did not mean his symptoms were imaginary. Context can alter real physiology and behavior. It meant the work cue carried information.

For another person, there is no such boundary. The low mood, self-criticism, sleep disruption, and loss of interest continue through weekends, vacations, and changes of task. That wider spread deserves a different level of concern.

Do not demand a perfect boundary. Severe occupational stress can spill into sleep, relationships, and physical health. The question is whether the work connection remains unusually strong and whether some parts of the self are more available when work demand is truly removed.

Fixing Yourself Can Hide a Job Problem

Burnout advice often moves quickly toward individual coping: breathing exercises, morning routines, gratitude, better nutrition, or resilience training. Some personal practices can make a hard season more manageable. They cannot create missing staff, remove impossible deadlines, stop harassment, correct unsafe workloads, or restore control that a role systematically denies.

Ben worked for a company where three people left and no one was replaced. His workload doubled, his manager praised his "ownership," and every missed deadline became a conversation about prioritization. Ben responded by becoming more efficient. For several months that helped the organization more than it helped him.

A work-focused analysis asks concrete questions. What demand increased? What control decreased? What resource disappeared?

Which expectations are contradictory? What happens if one demand is removed? Those questions do not assume that leaving the job is possible or wise. They make the environment visible.

Rest Is Part of Recovery, Not Proof

A break that reduces symptoms can support the idea that work demand matters. It cannot prove occupational burnout. People with depression, sleep debt, illness, and ordinary overwork can also feel better with rest.

Likewise, failure to recover during a weekend does not prove depression. Chronic strain can take longer than forty-eight hours to ease, and autistic burnout may involve a much deeper loss of capacity. The popular "vacation test" asks a useful observation question and then gives it too much authority.

A better approach is to notice the sequence. What improves first? Does dread fall before energy rises? Does interest return outside work? Does sleep change? How quickly do symptoms return when the work cues return? Record what happens instead of grading the break as a pass or fail.

Work Specificity Is a Guardrail

The World Health Organization's ICD-11 description keeps burnout inside the occupational context. It describes burnout as an occupational phenomenon resulting from chronic workplace stress that has not been successfully managed, with exhaustion, greater mental distance or cynicism toward the job, and reduced professional efficacy (World Health Organization, 2019). It also states that burnout should not be used to describe experiences in other areas of life.

That boundary is easy to lose in ordinary conversation. People say they are burned out on dating, parenting, politics, housework, or life itself. Those phrases communicate real strain. They do not automatically mean occupational burnout in the ICD-11 sense.

The distinction matters because a label can point attention in the wrong direction. If your exhaustion and loss of interest are broad, calling the entire pattern work burnout can encourage you to keep treating the job as the only cause. A change in job conditions may still help. It may simply be only one part of the picture.

Elena's pattern was strongly work-linked. She dreaded tasks, felt cynical toward work, and questioned whether anything she did there mattered. Yet she still felt warmth toward friends, interest in home projects, and relief when the work demand stopped. That does not prove burnout, but it matches the occupational shape better than a whole-life collapse.

Find the Work Mechanism

"Work is stressful" is often true and rarely specific enough to act on. Break the stress into mechanisms.

A workload problem means the amount or pace of work exceeds what can be done sustainably. A control problem means you have too little influence over priorities, methods, or timing. A values problem means the work repeatedly asks you to act against standards that matter to you. A fairness problem means effort and consequence are distributed in a way that feels persistently unjust. A social problem may involve conflict, harassment, isolation, or chronic unpredictability. A resource problem means you are responsible for outcomes without the staff, information, tools, authority, or time required to produce them.

The point is not to fit your job into a neat theory. It is to name what would have to change for the work to become more workable.

Consider two employees who both say, "I cannot face Monday." One is carrying the workload of two vacant posts. The other has manageable hours but spends every day under a manager who reverses decisions without warning and criticizes the result. A productivity system might help neither. Their problems require different conversations.

Write the sentence, "The part of work that is hardest to sustain is ______ because ______." If your answer is "everything," keep going until you can name at least one mechanism. Precision gives you something to test.

Improvement Outside Work Is Useful but Not Absolute

A common rule says that if you feel better on vacation, it is burnout, and if you do not, it is depression. That rule is too clean for real life.

First, a short break may not be enough to reverse months of exhaustion. Second, a person with depression can still have moments of relief or pleasure. Third, work burnout and depression can occur together. Fourth, an autistic person may leave the job but remain overloaded by travel, social demands, sensory exposure, and the effort of recovering from prolonged strain.

Use off-work change as one piece of evidence. Ask whether relief is predictable, what returns first, and what does not.

For example, professional cynicism may soften after several days away while sleep remains poor. That mixed response says more than "vacation helped." Interest in hobbies may return before energy. Or energy may rise while pleasure stays absent. Those sequences are worth recording because they show which dimensions move together and which do not.

Recovery Must Change the Source

Ben's first attempt at recovery was immaculate. He bought a sleep mask, blocked out Sunday afternoons, stopped drinking during the week, and followed a detailed morning routine. He became better rested and slightly more organized. By Wednesday afternoon he was still managing two jobs.

There is nothing wrong with sleep, exercise, food, or routines. The problem is using personal habits to compensate for a work system that keeps producing the same overload.

A work-focused recovery plan asks what can change in demand, control, support, role clarity, schedule, or expectations. Some changes are individual and modest, such as protecting a lunch break or declining an optional meeting. Others require management, accommodations, medical leave, a role change, collective action, or a decision to leave. Not every worker has equal leverage. Financial obligations, immigration status, caregiving, health insurance, discrimination, and labor conditions can sharply limit choices.

That reality is another reason to avoid moral language. Staying in a bad job is not evidence that someone wants burnout. Leaving is not always safe or possible. The goal is to identify the problem accurately enough that available choices are directed at the actual source.

Use a Work Off-Work Comparison

For seven days, choose one work demand and one nonwork activity with similar effort. Do not compare a difficult presentation with lying in bed. Compare tasks that ask something comparable of attention, movement, or social interaction.

You might compare an hour of writing reports with an hour planning a personal project. Compare a team meeting with dinner among familiar people. Compare commuting through a noisy station with a similarly busy weekend outing.

Record three things after each: how hard it was to start, how much interest or aversion you felt during it, and how long recovery took. The comparison may show that work content is uniquely aversive. It may show that every demanding activity has become difficult. It may reveal that sensory or social load, rather than the category "work," predicts the cost.

The value is in the pattern, not the score.

Know What Burnout Language Cannot Do

Burnout can be a useful occupational description. It cannot tell you whether you also meet criteria for a depressive disorder. It cannot rule out a medical cause of fatigue. It cannot explain every loss of function in an autistic person. And because burnout is not classified by WHO as a medical condition, telling a doctor only "I have burnout" may leave clinically important symptoms hidden behind a label (World Health Organization, 2019).

Bring the details instead. "I have become intensely cynical toward work, I recover somewhat on days off, and I still enjoy my family" is useful. "I have stopped enjoying everything, not only work" is useful. "I cannot tolerate meetings, shopping, or conversation because sensory and social demand has become much harder" is useful.

Labels are shorthand. The pattern is the evidence.

Principles to Remember

Occupational burnout has a work boundary in its formal definition. The symptoms can spill outside work, but the occupational context is not optional.

Use that boundary as a question, not a verdict. Look for job-linked exhaustion, cynicism or distance, reduced professional efficacy, and changes that track meaningful changes in work demand. Then look for what does not fit. Whole-life loss of interest, persistent hopelessness, major appetite or sleep changes, and safety concerns deserve assessment rather than being folded automatically into "just burnout."

A job can be the main problem. A mental disorder can be present at the same time. The next chapter turns to the pattern that most needs protection from the phrase "just stress": depression.

Chapter 3: Depression Crosses Contexts

There was nothing wrong with Nora's Saturday.

No alarm. No inbox. No difficult relative calling. The weather was mild, the house was quiet, and two friends had invited her to a lunch she normally liked. She stood in the kitchen looking at a clean mug and could not find a reason to make coffee.

The important detail was not that she felt tired. It was that the things which usually pulled her toward the day had stopped pulling. Work had been stressful for months, but the flatness no longer respected the edge of work.

Depressive disorders are not defined by exhaustion alone. Common features include persistent low or irritable mood, loss of interest or pleasure, sleep and appetite changes, low energy, difficulty concentrating, guilt or low self-worth, hopelessness, and thoughts about death or suicide. A depressive episode involves a pattern lasting most of the day, nearly every day, for at least two weeks, with meaningful distress or impairment (World Health Organization, 2025).

Chapter principle: Depression can include the same fatigue and concentration problems people call burnout, but its pattern is broader than a work reaction. Loss of interest or pleasure, changes in self-evaluation, persistence across settings, and safety concerns are especially important reasons to seek clinical assessment.

Tired Is Not the Same as Depressed

A person can be profoundly tired without having depression. A person can also have depression without describing the experience as sadness. Some people lead with irritability, numbness, slowing, sleep changes, poor concentration, physical heaviness, or a sense that nothing will matter.

This is one reason "But I'm not sad" does not rule depression out. It is also why a clinician asks about more than mood.

Grace described herself as "burned to a crisp" because that label felt less frightening. When she finally wrote down the changes, the list was larger: she had stopped playing the piano, ignored messages from people she loved, lost weight without trying, slept at odd times, and believed she was failing everyone. None of those facts diagnoses depression on a page. Together they make "only a work problem" harder to defend.

Interest Is Information

Loss of interest or pleasure is often called anhedonia. The word can sound technical, but the everyday question is simple: what happens when something you normally care about becomes available?

This is not a demand to enjoy yourself. People under heavy stress can lose access to hobbies because they have no time or energy. Autistic burnout can make desired activities inaccessible because processing and functional capacity have fallen. The useful distinction is not "Do hobbies fix you?" It is "What happened to wanting, pleasure, and capacity?"

Talia still wanted to garden. She ordered seeds and watched videos about tomatoes, then found that the physical and planning demands of planting were beyond her that week. The wanting remained visible. Jonah had time, tools, and a garden he had loved for years, but the whole subject felt empty. Again, neither detail settles a diagnosis. The difference is worth putting in the record.

Self-Evaluation Can Change

Occupational burnout can make someone feel ineffective at work. Depression may change the way a person evaluates themselves across roles.

Aisha did not only think, "I'm bad at my job." She thought she was a bad partner because she was quiet, a bad daughter because she had missed a call, and a bad friend because she had not answered a message. Small mistakes became evidence for a global case against herself.

Excessive guilt, worthlessness, and hopelessness are clinically important features in depression. When the mind begins turning ordinary limits into broad moral conclusions, it is worth saying that out loud to a professional rather than translating it into "I need a vacation."

Depression Has Treatments

The purpose of recognizing a depressive pattern is not to frighten yourself with a label. It is to open access to assessment and treatment.

World Health Organization guidance describes effective psychological treatments and medications for depression, with treatment choices depending on severity, circumstances, and clinical judgment. Major guidelines also include approaches such as cognitive behavioral therapy, behavioral activation, interpersonal psychotherapy, and antidepressant medication among treatment options (World Health Organization, 2025; Department of Veterans Affairs & Department of Defense, 2022; National Institute for Health and Care Excellence, 2022).

Behavioral activation deserves special care in a book about burnout. It does not mean "push through exhaustion until you feel better." In depression treatment it is a structured approach that examines the link between avoidance and mood and helps a person plan activities that can reconnect them with reinforcement and functioning. It is tailored, monitored, and adjusted. Turning that into a slogan about getting off the sofa misses the method (Department of Veterans Affairs & Department of Defense, 2022).

Safety Changes the Timeline

Some questions should not wait for a perfect differential.

If you are having thoughts of suicide, feel unable to keep yourself safe, or think you may act on self-harm thoughts, seek urgent help. In the United States, the 988 Suicide & Crisis Lifeline is available around the clock by call or text; in a life-threatening emergency, use local emergency services. Elsewhere, use the emergency or crisis service for your location (Substance Abuse and Mental Health Services Administration, 2025).

You do not need to decide whether the thoughts came from burnout, depression, autistic burnout, or an unbearable situation before asking for help. Safety is not a diagnostic reward you earn after answering every question correctly.

The Whole-Life Map

Take the timeline from Chapter 1 and add five domains: work, relationships, ordinary care tasks, interests or pleasure, and self-evaluation.

You are not looking for perfection. You are looking for spread. Does the problem remain mostly concentrated around work? Has it moved into nearly every domain? Are there islands of interest that remain available when demand drops? Has your view of your own worth changed? Are sleep, appetite, or movement noticeably different?

Write concrete observations. "I haven't played music in six weeks" is easier to assess than "nothing feels right." "I enjoy my daughter once I'm with her, but initiating plans feels impossible" carries different information than "being with anyone feels empty."

Depression Is More Than Low Mood

Depression can be mistaken for ordinary sadness because sadness is the symptom people recognize first. The clinical picture is broader.

The World Health Organization describes a depressive episode as involving depressed mood or loss of pleasure or interest for most of the day, nearly every day, for at least two weeks, with other symptoms that can include poor concentration, guilt or low self-worth, hopelessness, sleep disturbance, appetite or weight change, thoughts of death or suicide, and low energy (World Health Organization, 2025).

That list is not a home diagnostic checklist. It is a reminder that depression is a pattern involving duration, breadth, associated symptoms, and impairment.

Nora did not arrive at assessment because she had found the right label. She arrived because her whole-life pattern had changed. She had stopped wanting lunch with friends, stopped reading fiction, slept badly, struggled to eat, and felt that her future had narrowed. Work was difficult too, but work was no longer a special case.

The useful signal was spread.

Separate Pleasure From Performance

A person can perform while depressed. This is one reason the phrase "but I am still functioning" can delay care.

Performance may continue because bills must be paid, children need collecting, colleagues are relying on you, or years of habit keep a routine moving. The question is not only whether you can complete tasks. Ask what happens internally before, during, and after them.

Can you anticipate pleasure? Can you experience it while the activity is happening? Does satisfaction register afterward? Do you still care about outcomes that used to matter? Are you participating because you want to, or because stopping feels impossible?

These questions are not exclusive to depression, but they make anhedonia, the loss of interest or pleasure associated with depression, easier to describe. "I went to the concert" tells a clinician that you attended. "I went because the ticket was paid for, felt nothing while I was there, and wanted to leave the whole time" tells a different story.

The goal is not to inspect every moment for enjoyment. It is to notice a sustained change in your usual pattern.

Negative Conclusions Can Feel Like Facts

Depression can change the way a person evaluates the self, the future, and ordinary difficulty. A missed deadline may become "I ruin everything." A quiet weekend may become "Nobody wants me around." An uncertain career may become "Nothing will ever improve."

Do not argue with yourself as if you can win by force. Record the conclusion and ask whether it has become broader, harsher, and more final than your usual thinking. If so, include that change when you seek care.

This matters in the burnout differential because work burnout can also produce cynicism and reduced professional efficacy. The content helps. "This workplace is pointless" is different from "I am pointless." "I cannot keep doing this role" is different from "I cannot do anything right anywhere." The difference is not perfect, and both can coexist, but the scope of the judgment is useful information.

Treatment Is Not a Moral Test

People sometimes resist the possibility of depression because they hear it as a verdict about resilience. Others cling to a burnout explanation because changing jobs feels more concrete than considering mental health treatment. Neither reaction helps the differential.

Depression has evidence-based treatments. WHO and major clinical guidelines include psychological treatments, with medication used in appropriate circumstances depending on severity, preferences, prior response, and clinical assessment (World Health Organization, 2025; National Institute for Health and Care Excellence, 2022; Department of Veterans Affairs & Department of Defense, 2022).

Treatment is not proof that you were weak. Improvement after treatment is not proof that work conditions were fine. A person can be depressed in a damaging job. A person can need both treatment and a change in demand.

The practical question is what combination of assessment, support, and environmental change fits the actual pattern.

Make a Whole-Life Function Note

Use five areas: work, home tasks, relationships, pleasure or interest, and basic body routines such as sleep and eating. For each, write one sentence describing what has changed from your own baseline.

Avoid ratings like "good" or "bad." Use behavior.

"Work: I need twice as long to start routine tasks."

"Home: laundry waits for a week, even on days off."

"Relationships: I decline invitations I used to look forward to."

"Interest: I can watch a favorite show, but I do not care what happens."

"Body: I wake two hours earlier than usual and cannot return to sleep."

This is more useful than asking whether you "feel depressed enough." It also helps you notice when the picture is not global. Perhaps work is severely impaired while pleasure and relationships remain intact. Perhaps home and work are both difficult, but one sensory task is the strongest predictor. The map does not decide the diagnosis. It tells you what question to take forward.

Safety Is Part of the Differential

Thoughts about death or suicide change the priority. They are not something to postpone while you finish deciding whether the cause is burnout.

If you are in the United States and you are struggling or having thoughts of suicide, you can call or text 988 to reach the 988 Suicide & Crisis Lifeline. If you are in immediate danger, use emergency services (Substance Abuse and Mental Health Services Administration, 2025). Outside the United States, use local crisis or emergency services.

You do not need to settle the label before seeking help. The clinician can work on the differential while also addressing safety.

Do Not Dismiss a Short Improvement

Daniel felt much better for three hours when an old friend visited, then returned to the same flatness that evening. He took the improvement as evidence that he could not be depressed. That was too strong a conclusion.

Mood and interest can vary within depression. A good conversation, a deadline ending, better sleep, or a change of setting can matter. The diagnostic question is about the broader pattern over time, not whether one good moment occurred.

The opposite mistake happens too. One terrible Sunday does not prove depression when a person is facing Monday after months of unsustainable work. Look at duration, spread, associated symptoms, and function.

The aim is to give your clinician a time series, not a highlight reel.

In a Nutshell

Depression is not simply burnout that has become severe, and burnout is not simply mild depression. The research relationship between the two is debated, while clinical care still needs a careful account of mood, interest, duration, impairment, context, and safety.

If exhaustion has spread across your life, especially with persistent loss of interest or pleasure, hopelessness, strong guilt or worthlessness, major sleep or appetite change, or thoughts of death, move the question toward clinical assessment. You can still examine the role of work. You do not have to choose between taking the workplace seriously and taking depression seriously.

Chapter 4: Autistic Burnout Is Different

Samir could still do his job on paper.

He could log in, open the ticket system, and type answers that looked normal to anyone reading them later. What had changed was the cost. A video meeting that once required half an hour of recovery now took most of the afternoon. Grocery shopping became impossible after work. He stopped answering the phone because forming speech under surprise felt physically effortful. The blender, office lighting, and neighbor's music all seemed louder than before.

When he took leave, the job pressure stopped, but his capacity did not spring back. Quiet helped. Fewer decisions helped. Predictable days helped. Recovery was measured less by feeling cheerful than by being able to tolerate more input without losing function.

Autistic burnout is a developing research concept, not a formal diagnosis in the same way as major depressive disorder. In a foundational qualitative study, autistic adults described a pattern of long-term exhaustion, loss of skills, and reduced tolerance to stimulus associated with sustained demands that outstripped resources. Later qualitative and measurement research has developed the concept further (Raymaker et al., 2020; Mantzalas et al., 2022, 2024).

Chapter principle: Autistic burnout is best treated here as an evidence-informed pattern that may help organize observations, not as a self-diagnosis. Loss of functional capacity, increased sensory difficulty, cumulative demand, and masking history can add information that the ordinary burnout-versus-depression question misses.

The Research Is Younger

There is an important difference in evidence maturity.

Depressive disorders have extensive diagnostic and treatment research, established clinical guidelines, and long-standing systems of care. Occupational burnout has decades of organizational research and an ICD-11 definition as an occupational phenomenon. Autistic burnout has a smaller, newer body of research, much of it built with autistic participants and lived-experience accounts.

That does not make the concept imaginary. It means claims should match the evidence. Raymaker and colleagues' 2020 study helped define the pattern through qualitative work. Mantzalas and colleagues examined public posts and later worked on measurement and validation. The field is still refining how best to measure autistic burnout and how it relates to depression, anxiety, occupational burnout, and other forms of distress (Raymaker et al., 2020; Mantzalas et al., 2022, 2024).

A reader should therefore be suspicious of anyone offering a precise recovery timetable or a single diagnostic score as settled science.

Capacity Can Fall Unevenly

Autistic burnout accounts often emphasize reduced function. That can include difficulty with executive tasks, communication, self-care, sensory tolerance, or skills that were previously available.

Theo could still discuss the history of a favorite game for an hour but could not complete a form that required six unfamiliar steps. He worried that this inconsistency meant he was lazy. It meant only that capacity is not one tank with one gauge. Different tasks place different demands on language, sensory processing, initiation, switching, uncertainty, social performance, and working memory.

The same point matters in depression. A person can have severe depression and still perform selected tasks. Function is not an all-or-nothing test. The useful question is what changed relative to the person's own prior pattern and what kinds of demand now carry a much higher cost.

Masking Can Hide the Cost

Masking or camouflaging refers broadly to strategies autistic people may use to hide, compensate for, or manage visible autistic traits in social settings. The details and reasons vary widely. In autistic burnout research, sustained masking or camouflaging is commonly discussed as one contributor to cumulative load.

A person may look competent while spending far more internal effort than observers can see. That is why external performance can be a poor measure of remaining capacity.

Priya's colleagues saw a polished presenter. They did not see the hour she spent rehearsing a three-minute update, the lunch she skipped because the cafeteria was too loud, or the evening she spent in darkness after a client event. When she later lost the ability to maintain the same performance, people around her described the change as sudden. From her side, it was the end of a long accumulation.

The lesson is not that every autistic person masks or that masking always causes burnout. It is that visible competence does not tell you the price of competence.

Sensory Change Is Worth Recording

Increased sensory difficulty appears repeatedly in autistic burnout descriptions. Again, it is not a diagnostic test. Sensory sensitivity can fluctuate with stress, sleep, illness, migraine, anxiety, and other conditions.

Still, a sharp change can be informative. If ordinary lighting, sound, touch, movement, or social input has become harder to tolerate at the same time as functional capacity has fallen, record it.

Use comparisons instead of adjectives. "The supermarket was tiring before; now I leave after five minutes because the lights and overlapping voices become impossible to process" tells more than "I'm overstimulated." "I used to recover from a team meeting by lunch; now speech is difficult for the rest of the day" gives timing.

Reduction Is Not Surrender

When capacity is severely reduced, lowering demands can be a practical support. That may mean fewer decisions, less sensory input, more predictable routines, temporary reduction of social or work obligations, and assistance with tasks that currently cost too much.

This is where popular depression advice can collide with autistic burnout advice. Structured re-engagement can be useful in depression care. Demand reduction can be necessary when an autistic person has lost functional capacity. The conflict disappears when both approaches are individualized rather than turned into slogans.

No book can tell you the correct level of activity for your situation. If depression is present, a mental health professional can help determine how rest, routine, activity, and treatment fit together. If autistic burnout is part of the picture, accommodations and demand reduction may need to be included rather than treated as avoidance to be eliminated.

Autistic Burnout Has a Different Evidence Base

Autistic burnout is widely discussed in autistic communities, but its research base is newer than the evidence base for depressive disorders. That difference deserves respect rather than overconfidence.

In a participatory study, Raymaker and colleagues described autistic burnout through themes of chronic exhaustion, loss of skills, and reduced tolerance to stimulus, with contributing factors including chronic life stress and a mismatch between expectations and abilities without adequate support (Raymaker et al., 2020). Later qualitative and measurement work has continued to examine the construct and how it might be assessed (Mantzalas et al., 2022, 2024). A 2025 systematic review synthesized 48 studies and reported recurring experiences of debilitating exhaustion and increased disability, with sensory and social overwhelm and camouflaging among the reported contributors (Ali et al., 2025).

That is enough to take the phenomenon seriously. It is not enough to turn an online checklist into a diagnostic instrument. The term is not a substitute for assessment of depression, physical illness, sleep problems, medication effects, or other causes of a change in function.

A useful stance is, "This pattern resembles published descriptions of autistic burnout, and I want the alternatives considered too."

Loss of Access Can Look Like Loss of Desire

Samir still wanted to see his brother. The problem was that the train, restaurant noise, unpredictable conversation, and trip home had become a chain of demands he could no longer absorb. When his brother visited quietly at Samir's apartment, the desire to connect was obvious.

That distinction is not always clean, but it is important. Depression can involve loss of interest or pleasure. Autistic burnout may involve wanting an activity while lacking the current capacity to tolerate the sensory, social, executive, or communication demands around it.

Ask what happens when you reduce the cost without removing the activity.

If conversation is hard, is text easier? If shopping is impossible, does delivery restore enough capacity to cook? If the office is unbearable, does remote work change the picture? If social plans are too much, does meeting one familiar person in a quiet place feel different?

A change after accommodation is not proof of autistic burnout. It can show that the barrier is partly demand-sensitive.

Skills Can Become Less Available

People often describe burnout as being too tired to do things. Autistic burnout accounts often include something more specific: abilities that were previously available become less reliable or require far more effort. Research participants have described loss of skills and reduced capacity as part of the experience (Raymaker et al., 2020).

The practical task is to describe the change without turning it into a character judgment.

Instead of, "I have become lazy," write, "I used to make phone calls without planning them, and now I need a script and often cannot speak when the call is unexpected."

Instead of, "I am antisocial," write, "I still want contact, but after thirty minutes of conversation I lose track of words and need several hours without speech."

Instead of, "I cannot cope with anything," write, "I can complete familiar one-step tasks, but switching between tasks has become much harder."

Those sentences give a clinician a functional pattern to assess.

Sensory Tolerance Can Move Before You Notice It

The first sign is not always collapse. It may be that the office lights feel sharper, the dishwasher suddenly sounds unbearable, clothing seams are harder to ignore, or a familiar commute requires headphones and recovery. Someone who has spent years overriding sensory discomfort may interpret this as irritability rather than a change in sensory tolerance.

Keep the observation concrete. Which stimulus? In which setting? What happens in your body or behavior? Does reducing the stimulus help immediately, later, or not at all?

This is particularly useful when work and autistic burnout overlap. An open-plan office can produce both occupational strain and high sensory demand. Changing jobs to another open-plan office may remove one manager and preserve the same sensory load. A more precise account changes what solutions are considered.

Masking Can Hide the External Signal

A person may appear "fine" precisely because they are spending more resources on appearing fine.

Masking, or camouflaging autistic traits in social settings, can include monitoring facial expression, rehearsing language, suppressing movements, copying conversational styles, and forcing tolerance of environments that are costly. Raymaker and colleagues' participants described masking and lack of support among factors connected with burnout (Raymaker et al., 2020).

You do not need to prove how much you mask. Ask what you do to make interactions look easier than they are.

Theo arrives early so he can rehearse the first sentence of a meeting. Grace studies everyone's faces to decide when to laugh. Aisha remains at a team dinner for two hours, then spends the next day unable to speak much. From the outside, all three events may look successful.

The differential question is not whether the performance worked. It is what it cost.

Accommodation Is a Test of Demand, Not Identity

People sometimes think they must be certain they are autistic before trying anything that reduces sensory or communication demand. Many low-risk adjustments do not require that certainty.

Written agendas, predictable schedules, quieter workspaces, ear protection where safe, reduced unnecessary social exposure, more recovery time between demands, and help with high-step household tasks can be evaluated by function. Do they reduce cost? Do they restore access to activities you value? Do they make capacity more predictable?

Where workplace accommodations require formal documentation, the process depends on local law and employer policy, so professional or legal guidance may be needed. The broader principle is simpler: if a demand can be reduced safely, the response may teach you something about what was consuming capacity.

Keep Depression in the Picture

Autistic people can also experience depression. Autistic burnout does not protect someone from a depressive disorder, and depression should not be assumed to be merely an autistic trait or an inevitable part of being autistic.

If low mood, loss of interest or pleasure, hopelessness, appetite or sleep changes, thoughts of death, or whole-life impairment are present, bring them to a clinician even if the autistic burnout explanation feels compelling. Depression has established treatments, and missing it because another label feels more personally accurate can delay help.

The safest differential does not ask which label wins. It asks which problems need attention at the same time.

Principles to Remember

Autistic burnout gives us a third pattern to consider when "burnout or depression?" is too small a question. The research points toward long-term exhaustion, reduced function or skills, and lower tolerance for input or demand, often in the context of sustained mismatch between demands and resources.

Treat those features as observations, not a home diagnosis. Record changes in speech, executive function, self-care, sensory tolerance, social capacity, and recovery time. Note the role of masking and cumulative demands if they are relevant to you.

Most importantly, allow overlap. An autistic person can be depressed. An autistic employee can have occupational burnout. Autistic burnout can sit beside either. The next chapters introduce a way to examine those possibilities without forcing the answer into a single box.

Chapter 5: The Three Question Check

A useful differential starts by slowing down the urge to name the problem.

Most people do the opposite. They collect symptoms until one label feels familiar, then reinterpret everything through that label. If they choose burnout, the low mood becomes "just exhaustion." If they choose depression, every work trigger becomes evidence that the disorder is making work feel worse. If they choose autistic burnout, every shutdown or lost skill may be folded into that explanation.

The Three Question Check is designed to interrupt that loop. It is not a screening tool and it has no score. It asks three ordinary questions that organize information before you decide what the information means.

Chapter principle: Ask about context, capacity, and change. Where does the pattern live? What exactly has become less available? What changes when demands, support, activity, or setting change? The value lies in the pattern across all three questions, not in any single answer.

Question One Is Context

Context asks where the problem is strongest and how it began.

Did symptoms rise alongside a change in workload, control, staffing, conflict, values, schedule, or job security? Do they intensify when work cues appear? Are there meaningful periods away from work when parts of your usual interest or functioning return?

Then widen the view. What happens in relationships, hobbies, ordinary care tasks, and quiet time? Does the same flatness or hopelessness show up everywhere? Are there sensory or social environments that have become much harder than before? Did the change follow months or years of sustained masking, transitions, caregiving, or other cumulative demand?

Context is not only place. It includes timing. A pattern that began after a promotion and tracks every escalation in workload carries different information from one that began during a quiet period and spread steadily across life.

Question Two Is Capacity

Capacity asks what is missing.

There is a practical difference between "I want to, but I cannot mobilize the function" and "I have no interest in it anymore." Real life is not binary, and both can happen together, but the distinction gives a clinician something to work with.

Ask about initiation, planning, switching, language, sensory tolerance, social effort, physical energy, pleasure, curiosity, and emotional range. Which abilities have become unreliable? Which interests remain alive but inaccessible? Which activities can you still do once someone else removes the planning burden?

Maya, from the introduction, noticed that music still mattered to her. She kept saving albums to a playlist. She simply could not tolerate sound after work. That was different from a period years earlier when music had felt emotionally blank. The comparison did not diagnose either period. It sharpened the description.

Question Three Is Change

Change asks what moves the pattern.

A real reduction in work demand may lower dread and cynicism. Quiet and reduced sensory demand may restore a little communication or executive capacity. Structured activity may increase contact with pleasure or mastery in depression treatment. Sleep restoration can improve many forms of distress. Medical treatment can alter fatigue if a physical condition is contributing.

The important word is "may."

Do not turn your life into a set of harsh experiments. If you are severely depleted, the answer to "what happens if I push much harder?" may be obvious enough. Change can be observed through natural variations: weekends, leave, a quieter room, a cancelled obligation, help with errands, a day with social contact, a medication change supervised by a prescriber, or a period when work pressure eases.

Track what changes first and what does not.

The Questions Work Together

Suppose Daniel reports that his worst symptoms cluster around work, his interest in music returns during time off, and genuine removal of work demand lowers dread before it restores energy. Those observations lean toward a work-centered explanation without ruling out depression.

Suppose Nora reports that low mood and loss of pleasure continue at home, at work, and on vacation, that self-worth has fallen across roles, and that a quieter week does little to restore interest. Those observations make clinical assessment for depression more pressing.

Suppose Samir reports whole-life exhaustion after sustained cumulative demand, sharp loss of sensory tolerance and communication capacity, continuing interest in a few topics, and some improvement when sensory and social demands are reduced. That makes autistic burnout worth discussing, especially if he is autistic or undergoing an autism assessment, while still checking for depression and medical contributors.

The questions do not generate labels. They generate better evidence.

Beware of the Perfect Story

Human beings prefer coherent explanations. Illness and stress often refuse to provide one.

A person may have occupational burnout and major depression. An autistic person may have all three patterns at once. A job change may reduce one layer of distress while leaving a depressive episode untouched. Antidepressant treatment may improve mood while an impossible workload continues to exhaust the person. Accommodations may restore autistic capacity while grief remains.

If your answers point in different directions, that is not failure. Mixed answers are common enough to deserve their own chapter.

Write the Three Sentences

Before you move on, try a first version of the Three Question Check in exactly three sentences.

For context: "This began around ___, is worst when ___, and also affects ___."

For capacity: "I still want or care about ___, but I struggle to ___; I have also lost interest or pleasure in ___."

For change: "When ___ changes, I notice ___ improves or worsens first, while ___ stays the same."

Do not polish the sentences. The gaps and contradictions are useful.

What a Good Differential Question Does

A good question separates plausible explanations without pretending that the answer is absolute. "Am I tired?" is a poor differential question because all three patterns in this book can include exhaustion. "Do I hate my job?" is also weak because depression can make work feel unbearable and a damaging job can make anyone hate going in.

The Three Question Check is designed around pattern rather than symptom count:

Context: Where is the change strongest, and where is it noticeably different?

Capacity: What has become unavailable, and is the problem desire, access, endurance, sensory tolerance, executive effort, or professional confidence?

Change: What shifts when relevant conditions change, and what stays?

Each question has limits. Context can be blurred when work invades home. Capacity can be hard to describe when several problems happen at once. Change can mislead when recovery is slow. The strength comes from using all three together.

Context Needs Contrast

Suppose Priya says, "I am exhausted everywhere." That sounds like whole-life spread. Then she notices that on days without meetings she can cook, read, and call her sister. On meeting-heavy days, she cannot tolerate conversation after 6 p.m. The exhaustion is broad in location but linked to a specific demand.

Now suppose Daniel says, "Work makes me worse." That sounds occupational. But on leave he remains unable to enjoy music, food, friends, or sleep, and his hopelessness does not lift. Work may be an aggravating factor without being the whole explanation.

Context therefore includes time, demand, and setting, not just place.

Ask: What predicts the difficult period? What reliably comes before it? What is different on a better day? What remains even when the obvious stressor is gone?

A contrast is more informative than a label.

Capacity Needs Components

"Functioning" sounds like one switch. In practice it is a bundle.

You may have physical energy but no tolerance for noise. You may want connection but struggle to produce speech. You may be able to work but not handle household steps. You may complete tasks while feeling no pleasure. You may think clearly about a favorite topic but be unable to initiate a routine email.

Break capacity into parts: initiation, attention, switching, memory, communication, sensory tolerance, social endurance, self-care tasks, movement, and pleasure or interest. You do not need to track all of them. Choose the two or three that changed most.

The question "What exactly cannot happen now?" is much more useful than "How bad is my functioning?"

Change Needs a Plausible Mechanism

A week off feels like a strong experiment because the variable appears simple. It is not. During a week off you may sleep more, receive fewer emails, commute less, spend less time masking, encounter less sensory input, eat differently, see different people, and feel less time pressure. If you improve, several mechanisms could explain it.

Make the change smaller when you can.

If meetings are the suspected driver, reduce or cluster meetings if your role allows it and watch what changes. If sensory demand is suspected, adjust one predictable source. If the problem is broad loss of pleasure and low mood, do not use more rest as a home diagnostic test. Bring the pattern to a clinician.

The Three Question Check is not about proving causation. It is about making the next hypothesis more precise.

A Worked Example

Grace is a project manager who has spent four months saying she is burned out. She is exhausted, behind on household tasks, and withdrawing from friends.

Context: She is worst after two consecutive office days. On quiet weekends, she wants to see one close friend but cannot manage a busy restaurant. Work is a major demand, yet the cost follows her into other settings.

Capacity: She still wants her hobbies. The strongest changes are speech under pressure, tolerance for fluorescent light and layered sound, and switching between tasks. She can read a novel if the room is quiet. She cannot follow a group conversation after work.

Change: Remote days help more than weekends alone. Written communication is easier than spontaneous calls. Ear protection makes the commute less costly. A three-day break improves some physical tiredness but not the new sensory sensitivity.

The pattern does not establish autistic burnout. It gives a clinician specific reasons to consider autistic burnout alongside occupational burnout, depression, and other contributors.

Now change one detail. Suppose Grace says she no longer wants the novel, the friend, the meal, or anything else she previously enjoyed, and this stays true on quiet remote days. Depression becomes more important to assess.

The Three Question Check is doing its job when one changed detail meaningfully changes the questions.

The Check Also Finds Mixed Patterns

Marcus answers the three questions this way:

Context: the decline began during a prolonged work crisis, but low mood now continues away from work.

Capacity: work initiation is terrible, and pleasure has also fallen across hobbies and relationships.

Change: a two-week leave reduced dread and cynicism, but sleep, appetite, interest, and hopelessness barely changed.

A simplistic burnout test might stop at "leave helped." A simplistic depression test might ignore that removing work demand clearly improved one part of the picture. The combined answer is, "There may be more than one process here."

That sentence can prevent a false either-or decision.

Write for a Clinician, Not an Algorithm

Online self-tests reward complete answers. Clinical conversations often begin with uncertainty.

Try writing three sentences that could survive outside your private theory:

"Context: This began after six months of increased workload, but in the last eight weeks it has spread into weekends."

"Capacity: I can still enjoy my children when I am with them, but I cannot start ordinary tasks and I have stopped wanting most hobbies."

"Change: A week away from work reduced dread, but my sleep and low mood did not improve."

Those sentences do not ask a clinician to agree with a diagnosis. They give the clinician observations that can be examined.

Do Not Optimize the Answers

Once people learn a differential, there is a temptation to produce a cleaner case. Someone who wants the burnout explanation notices every good Saturday. Someone who fears depression edits out a moment of pleasure. Someone who has finally found language for autistic burnout may interpret every difficult interaction as sensory overload.

Write contradictory evidence down too.

"I felt much better on Tuesday even though work was busy."

"I enjoyed dinner despite feeling low all day."

"The quiet room did not help this time."

Contradictions do not ruin your case. They protect you from fitting your life to a label.

In a Nutshell

The Three Question Check does not replace assessment. It gives assessment better material.

Context shows where and when the pattern takes shape. Capacity distinguishes among kinds of loss that are often collapsed into "no motivation." Change shows which parts of the pattern are sensitive to demand, support, activity, setting, or time.

You will spend the next three chapters examining each question more carefully. Keep your answers provisional. A good differential gets clearer because it tolerates uncertainty long enough to gather the information that certainty would hide.

Chapter 6: Context Shows the Pattern

The office was nearly empty when Marcus noticed the contradiction.

He had spent the morning unable to write a two-paragraph proposal. Every sentence felt impossible. At lunch, a colleague asked about a neighborhood planning dispute Marcus had followed for years. He spoke for twenty minutes without losing the thread.

The contrast irritated him. If his brain worked for one topic, why did it fail for the document that paid his salary?

Because "can concentrate" is not a single setting-free ability. Interest, threat, fatigue, sensory load, task ambiguity, social evaluation, and meaning all alter what a person can access. Context does not tell you the diagnosis, but it can reveal structure hidden by a global phrase such as "my brain is gone."

Chapter principle: Map symptoms against settings and demands before treating them as universal. Occupational burnout should have a meaningful work connection. Depression can cross settings. Autistic burnout may be tied to cumulative demand that spans work and nonwork life. Context makes those differences visible.

Start With Onset, Not Memory

When people are exhausted, the past compresses. Six months can feel like "forever." Try anchoring onset to external events.

When did someone else first notice a change? When did you begin missing deadlines, cancelling plans, sleeping differently, or needing much longer to recover? Was there a job reorganization, bereavement, illness, move, relationship change, caregiving burden, medication change, or period of intense masking around the same time?

Do not assume the nearby event caused the problem. The purpose is chronological.

Grace initially said her exhaustion began "during a bad year." When she checked her calendar, she saw two phases. Work dread began after her team lost staff in March. Loss of interest in friends and food appeared months later, after sleep had deteriorated. That sequence raised the possibility that a work problem had been followed by something broader.

Work Specificity Matters

Because WHO restricts burn-out to the occupational context, a work link is more than a convenient clue. It is part of the concept (World Health Organization, 2019).

Ask how you feel before, during, and after contact with work. Notice specific cues. Is Sunday evening different from Saturday morning? Does energy change after a meeting with one manager? Are symptoms strongest during high-control tasks, low-control tasks, customer contact, sensory-heavy environments, or work that conflicts with your values?

Then ask what remains intact outside work. The answer does not have to be "everything." Severe work stress often follows people home. Look for relative differences.

Elena, from Chapter 2, still had access to laughter and hands-on activity away from the spreadsheet. That did not mean she was healthy. It meant some systems were more available in another context.

Whole-Life Spread Matters Too

Depression can affect functioning across work, home, social life, sleep, appetite, interest, and self-evaluation. WHO describes depressive episodes as involving depressed mood or loss of interest or pleasure along with other symptoms, generally present most of the day, nearly every day, for at least two weeks (World Health Organization, 2025).

A broad pattern is not automatically depression. Physical illnesses, grief, trauma, chronic pain, sleep disorders, medication effects, and other conditions can also spread across settings. The point is that whole-life spread weakens a purely occupational explanation.

Luis realized this when he took a week away from work and still could not enjoy a long-planned visit from his brother. The work dread disappeared. The flatness did not. That difference was exactly the kind of information his doctor needed.

Cumulative Demand Crosses Categories

Autistic burnout complicates the simple work-versus-life map because the load may be cumulative across domains.

Aisha's paid job was manageable in isolation. So was parenting. So was a weekly medical appointment. So was the noisy train she used to reach the office. What became unmanageable was the combined load after months with almost no low-demand space.

Autistic burnout research describes the role of sustained life stress and mismatch between demands and available resources, with reports of exhaustion, reduced function, and reduced tolerance for stimulus (Raymaker et al., 2020; Mantzalas et al., 2022).

For an autistic person, therefore, "Does it go away when I stop working?" may be too narrow. Work may be one major contributor without being the only source of demand.

Make a Seven Day Context Map

For one week, keep notes that take less than two minutes.

At three points in the day, write where you are, what demand is active, and what is hardest. Include one concrete function: speech, concentration, initiation, sensory tolerance, pleasure, appetite, or physical energy.

You are not trying to produce a perfect dataset. You are looking for contrasts.

"Tuesday 8 a.m., before work, stomach tight, dread 8/10, could still enjoy podcast."

"Tuesday 7 p.m., home after three meetings, could not tolerate kitchen noise, wanted dinner but could not plan it."

"Saturday noon, no work contact, still no interest in seeing anyone, stayed in bed despite sleeping nine hours."

Those notes carry more information than a daily rating of "burnout 7."

Context Can Also Reveal Medical Clues

Some patterns do not fit the three labels well.

Fatigue that worsens with physical exertion, new shortness of breath, fainting, fever, unexpected weight change, heavy bleeding, new pain, marked snoring with daytime sleepiness, or symptoms after a medication change all deserve medical attention. The list is not complete. It is a reminder that exhaustion is not owned by psychology.

MedlinePlus lists many possible causes of fatigue, including anemia, sleep disorders, thyroid problems, depression, medicines, persistent pain, and substance use (MedlinePlus, 2025).

If your context map says, "This has no clear relationship to work, mood, interest, sensory load, or social demand, but it began after a physical change," take that seriously.

Context Has More Than One Scale

There are at least four useful scales of context: minute, day, week, and season.

At the minute scale, ask what happened immediately before a change. Was it a difficult email, a noisy shop, an unexpected conversation, a change in posture, or nothing obvious?

At the day scale, look for concentration of demand. Are mornings consistently better? Do you deteriorate after meetings? Are days off different before you even remember they are days off?

At the week scale, ask whether workdays and nonwork days separate. Does Sunday bring anticipatory dread? Does capacity recover after a quieter weekend, or does the pattern remain broadly unchanged?

At the seasonal scale, look for onset and persistence. Did this begin after a promotion, bereavement, illness, move, medication change, caregiving period, conflict, or months of cumulative overload? Depression and burnout can both follow stressful periods, so the event itself is not the diagnosis. It helps establish sequence.

A context map becomes more useful when it has time attached to it.

Home Is Not Automatically a Control Condition

People often compare work with home as if home were demand-free. It may not be.

A parent may finish an eight-hour shift and begin three hours of caregiving. A disabled person may spend nonwork time coordinating health care. An autistic person may leave a demanding office for a household full of sensory and social activity. Someone living alone may use the evening for every task the workday crowded out.

If you do not feel better at home, ask whether home actually removes the suspected demand.

This changes the interpretation of weekends too. A weekend filled with errands, family obligations, noise, travel, and unfinished work is not a clean test of what happens away from job stress.

The point is not to manufacture a perfect rest day. It is to notice which demands traveled with you.

Notice Anticipation and Recovery Separately

Elena felt better by Friday evening and worse by Sunday afternoon. At first she recorded Sunday as evidence that her symptoms were present outside work. Then she noticed what happened at 4 p.m.: she opened the calendar to check Monday's meetings.

Anticipation can pull work into nonwork time. That does not make the Sunday feeling unreal. It changes its context.

Likewise, recovery lag can make a work-linked problem last into Saturday. The fact that you are still exhausted twelve hours after leaving the office does not prove the exhaustion is unrelated to work.

Record both the trigger and the lag. "I start feeling dread when I see Monday's schedule" is different from "I wake with the same low mood every day, including during leave." "Noise tolerance returns after two quiet days" is different from "noise is equally difficult regardless of demand."

Whole-Life Spread Needs Careful Wording

When symptoms spread across contexts, people often jump to depression. Whole-life spread is important, but it is not exclusive to depression. Severe sleep deprivation, physical illness, caregiving strain, autistic burnout, medication effects, and prolonged work stress can all affect several parts of life.

Depression becomes more important to assess when spread is accompanied by its characteristic pattern, including sustained low mood or loss of interest or pleasure and associated symptoms over time (World Health Organization, 2025).

Autistic burnout becomes more important to consider when broad exhaustion comes with loss of skills and increased sensory sensitivity in an autistic person or someone being assessed for autism, while remembering that this construct has a developing evidence base (Raymaker et al., 2020; Mantzalas et al., 2022, 2024).

The map tells you where to look next. It does not provide the final answer.

Seven Days, Three Lines Per Day

A useful context log can be short enough to maintain.

At the end of each day write:

"Main demand: ______."

"Most noticeable change in capacity: ______."

"One thing that felt easier than expected, if anything: ______."

Add sleep or physical symptoms only if they are relevant to your question. Do not create a twenty-item tracker unless you know you will use it.

A week is often long enough to expose contrasts but too short to establish many clinical patterns. Treat the log as a snapshot. If the problem is persistent, continue only if the tracking is helping you communicate, not if it is turning into constant self-monitoring.

Context Can Reveal a Medical Route

Luis thought his fatigue was obviously stress because work had been difficult. His context log showed something odd: stairs were worse regardless of whether he was at work, home, or on leave. The exertion pattern mattered more than the location.

Fatigue can have many causes, and a medical differential may consider physical conditions, sleep, medications, substances, and mental health factors depending on the presentation (MedlinePlus, 2025, 2026). NIMH also notes that medical conditions and some medications can produce symptoms that resemble depression, and a health care provider may use history, examination, and tests as appropriate to rule out alternatives (National Institute of Mental Health, n.d.).

Context is therefore not only psychological. The body has context too: exertion, meals, menstrual cycle, infection, pain, medication timing, sleep, and other changes may matter.

A Better Onset Story

When a clinician asks, "When did this start?" do not worry if you cannot name a date. Use phases.

"Last autumn I was tired but functioning normally. Around January, after the second staff vacancy, I started dreading work and working more slowly. By March I was canceling plans after office days. In April, I noticed low mood on weekends too."

Or:

"I have always found noisy environments costly. Since a run of travel and social obligations in February, I need much longer to recover and I have lost access to tasks that used to be routine."

That kind of onset story makes sequence visible without pretending memory is exact.

Principles to Remember

Context is the geography and chronology of the problem.

A strong work connection supports a work-focused inquiry. Whole-life spread increases the importance of depression and medical assessment. Cumulative autistic demand may cross the work boundary entirely. Physical patterns can point outside all three.

Do not force a neat map. Write the contradictions down. "Work makes it much worse, but I am still flat on vacation" is valuable. "Quiet restores speech but not pleasure" is valuable. "I feel emotionally fine and physically exhausted after minimal exertion" is valuable.

The next question asks what has actually been lost, because "capacity" and "motivation" are not interchangeable words.

Chapter 7: Capacity Is Not Motivation

Talia wanted to answer the message.

She liked the person who had sent it. She had read it three times. She knew what she wanted to say. Yet each attempt to type the first line produced the same sense of too many moving parts: tone, timing, context, possible follow-up, one more social thread to keep open.

She put the phone down.

From the outside, this could look like avoidance, low motivation, depression, autistic overload, simple fatigue, or ordinary procrastination. From the inside, the most useful first question was smaller: what part of the task had become unavailable?

Chapter principle: Separate desire, pleasure, initiation, execution, and tolerance. When all are reduced to the word "motivation," important differences disappear. Capacity describes what you can reliably do under current conditions, not how much you care or how virtuous you are.

Wanting and Doing Can Split

People often judge themselves through outcomes. If the task did not happen, they conclude they did not want it enough.

That is poor measurement.

You can want dinner and be unable to plan, shop, cook, and clean. You can want company and be unable to tolerate conversation. You can care about work and be unable to sustain the executive load. You can also have enough physical ability to do something and find that interest or pleasure has disappeared.

Depression can involve loss of interest or pleasure. Autistic burnout research emphasizes reduced function and loss of skills. Occupational burnout can include reduced professional efficacy and detachment from work. Those are overlapping but not identical descriptions (World Health Organization, 2019, 2025; Raymaker et al., 2020).

Break Capacity Into Parts

When a task fails, ask where.

Initiation is getting started. Sequencing is knowing what comes next. Working memory is holding information while acting. Switching is moving between steps or tasks. Language is finding and producing words. Sensory tolerance is staying functional in the environment. Social capacity is managing interaction. Physical stamina is sustaining movement. Emotional reward is the sense that something is interesting, satisfying, or worth approaching.

These are not diagnostic categories. They are descriptive handles.

Jonah said he "couldn't cook anymore." The closer description was that he could cook if ingredients were already chosen and placed on the counter, but choosing a meal and entering a crowded store stopped the process. That suggested a planning and sensory bottleneck, not a loss of all cooking skill.

Nora's version was different. She could prepare food when necessary but felt no appetite and no pleasure in meals she used to enjoy. That was a different loss.

Loss of Skill Deserves Attention

Autistic adults in burnout research have described loss of skills or reduced ability to function, alongside exhaustion and lower tolerance for stimulus (Raymaker et al., 2020).

"Loss" does not always mean a skill has vanished permanently. It can mean access becomes unreliable or requires far more effort than before. A person who usually speaks fluidly may need more time, fewer words, text instead of speech, or silence after sustained demand.

A person who managed complex routines may need external support for simple sequencing.

Record the before-and-after comparison. "I used to take three phone calls in a morning and recover over lunch. Now one unplanned call can end my ability to speak comfortably for hours" is clinically and practically useful.

Anhedonia Is a Different Kind of Loss

In depression, loss of interest or pleasure is a central feature. WHO includes loss of pleasure or interest among core symptoms of depressive episodes (World Health Organization, 2025).

A common mistake is to assume that any failure to do enjoyable things is anhedonia. It may be. It may also be access.

Ask two questions. If the activity were magically made easy, would any pull toward it remain? If you do manage to begin, is there any pleasure, absorption, or relief once you are doing it?

These are observations, not diagnostic tests. Depression can coexist with preserved pockets of pleasure, and severe exhaustion can blunt pleasure temporarily. Still, the distinction helps you describe what has changed.

Professional Efficacy Is Narrower

Reduced professional efficacy in occupational burnout concerns work. A person can feel ineffective, detached, or cynical in the job while remaining competent and interested elsewhere.

Ben noticed he had started making mistakes in reports, avoiding decisions, and assuming every new project would fail. On weekends he still organized a local sports league with surprising energy. The contrast did not erase his exhaustion. It kept the work domain visible.

If Ben had generalized the conclusion "I am incapable" to parenting, friendships, finances, and basic self-worth, that broader change would deserve separate attention.

Use Assistance as Information

Support can reveal capacity that stress hides.

Try reducing one layer without increasing pressure elsewhere. Ask someone else to choose the meal while you cook. Move a meeting to audio-only if permitted. Use written communication instead of a spontaneous call. Work in a quieter room. Break an assignment into a single visible next step. Let a friend accompany you to a medical appointment.

If function returns when one demand is removed, record that. It tells you something about the bottleneck.

Do not interpret improvement as proof that the problem was "not serious." A ramp helping someone enter a building does not prove there was no access problem. Support changes the task.

A Capacity Inventory

Write five sentences beginning with different verbs.

"I want to..."

"I can still..."

"I can do this only if..."

"I used to be able to..."

"I no longer get pleasure from..."

The pattern may surprise you. You may find that desire is intact while execution has collapsed. You may find that ability is intact but interest has vanished. You may find that both are reduced.

Take the exact sentences with you when you seek assessment. They are more useful than calling yourself unmotivated.

Capacity Has a Shape

Two people can both say "I cannot do anything" and mean completely different things.

Talia can think, read, and solve a familiar technical problem. She cannot start a socially ambiguous message. Jonah can begin tasks but loses the thread after ten minutes. Maya can work for hours but has no capacity left to make food. Samir can plan what he wants to say but speech becomes difficult under unexpected social demand. Nora can complete routine tasks but experiences little interest or pleasure in any of them.

Each pattern calls for a different follow-up question.

The phrase "low functioning" hides all of that. Replace it with verbs: starting, switching, remembering, speaking, tolerating, deciding, enjoying, moving, sleeping, eating.

Desire Is Not a Reliable Shortcut Either

The distinction between "I want to but cannot" and "I do not want to" can be useful, especially when comparing access problems with loss of interest. It is not absolute.

A person with depression may want to want something. They may miss the idea of reading while feeling no pull toward the book. An autistic person in burnout may stop wanting a social event because the cost has become predictable. A burned-out worker may still care about the purpose of the profession while feeling disgust toward the current workplace.

Ask three versions instead:

"Do I anticipate any pleasure or meaning in this?"

"Can I access it once I begin?"

"What is the cost afterward?"

The three answers often carry more information than desire alone.

Professional Efficacy Is Domain-Specific

WHO includes reduced professional efficacy as one of the dimensions in its burnout description (World Health Organization, 2019). That is narrower than a global belief that you are incompetent.

A worker may think, "I am terrible at this job now," while still feeling competent as a parent, musician, friend, volunteer, or problem solver. Depression can involve low self-worth or guilt that reaches more broadly, though not every depressed person experiences it in the same way (World Health Organization, 2025).

Record the scope of the judgment. "I do not trust myself with client work anymore" is different from "I am a burden everywhere." Both deserve attention. They point to different lines of assessment.

Assistance Can Show Where the Bottleneck Is

A useful way to understand capacity is to remove one step.

Maya cannot cook after work. When groceries arrive preselected and chopped, she can cook. The bottleneck may be planning and task steps rather than appetite.

Samir cannot join a spontaneous meeting. With an agenda and written questions in advance, he can contribute. The bottleneck may be unpredictability and live communication demand.

Nora cannot make herself attend a movie alone. A friend collects her and she still experiences no pleasure while watching it. That does not diagnose depression, but removing initiation did not restore interest.

Assistance does not create a medical test. It makes the function more specific.

Capacity Changes Can Be Important Even When Performance Stays High

Marcus still hit every deadline. He did it by starting at 5 a.m., skipping lunch, and working Sunday. If you only measure output, his capacity looks intact.

A better measure includes the resources required to produce the output.

How much recovery is needed afterward? What other tasks disappear so one task can stay? How much preparation is required? Is the same output being bought with less sleep, more isolation, or increasingly rigid routines?

High performance can coexist with serious strain. The external result is one data point, not the whole function.

Build an Assistance Ladder

Choose one task that has become difficult. Write four versions from highest demand to lowest.

For a phone call:

1. Unexpected live call.
2. Scheduled live call.
3. Scheduled call with written agenda.
4. Written message instead.

For grocery shopping:

1. Busy store at an unpredictable time.
2. Quiet store with a fixed list.
3. Curbside pickup.
4. Delivery of a saved basket.

Try the lowest-risk version that is available to you. Notice whether capacity returns when the demand changes.

If every version remains difficult and the task belongs to a broader loss of interest, energy, or functioning, that is useful too. If one specific adjustment changes the task dramatically, record it.

Look for Unevenness

Autistic burnout descriptions often emphasize loss of skills and reduced tolerance to stimulus (Raymaker et al., 2020). One implication is that capacity may become unusually uneven. A person can do a complex familiar task while being unable to tolerate a simple but unpredictable one.

That unevenness is easy to judge from the outside. "You can work, so why can you not answer the phone?" "You can play a game for two hours, so why can you not clean the kitchen?"

Complexity and demand are not the same. A familiar absorbing task may have low switching, low social uncertainty, and controlled sensory input. A supposedly simple errand may require transitions, choices, noise, navigation, conversation, and recovery.

Describe the demand profile rather than arguing about which task "should" be harder.

Do Not Make Capacity a Verdict

The purpose of an inventory is not to decide what kind of person you have become.

Write, "Speech is less available under surprise," not "I am failing socially."

Write, "I need more recovery after meetings," not "I am weak."

Write, "Pleasure is absent from activities I usually like," not "I am ungrateful."

Clinical language is useful here because it can be less moral than everyday language. It turns a judgment into an observation that can be assessed.

In a Nutshell

Capacity is not character, and motivation is too broad a word for differential thinking.

Separate wanting from pleasure, initiation from execution, and skill from access. Occupational burnout may narrow efficacy and engagement around work. Depression can reduce interest or pleasure across life. Autistic burnout may involve a marked fall in functional and sensory capacity.

None of these differences is absolute. The value is descriptive. When you can say precisely what became hard, another person has a better chance of asking the right next question.

Chapter 8: Change Is Only a Clue

The most seductive question in burnout discussions is also one of the easiest to misuse: "Do you feel better after rest?"

It sounds scientific because it has a before and an after. It is not a diagnostic test.

A person with work burnout may improve when job demands are removed. A person with depression may also improve after sleep, safety, connection, treatment, or relief from an acute stressor. An autistic person in burnout may need substantial demand reduction and still recover slowly. A person with untreated anemia may feel exhausted in every setting regardless of how wisely they rest.

Chapter principle: Observe change, but do not force it into a pass-or-fail rule. The useful information is what shifts first, under which conditions, how much, and for how long.

What Rest Actually Changes

Rest is not one intervention.

Sleeping after severe sleep debt is different from spending a day scrolling while worried about work. Quiet sensory recovery is different from social withdrawal. A vacation filled with travel, decisions, family obligations, and unfamiliar environments may be less restorative for an autistic person than an ordinary low-demand week at home.

If you want to learn from rest, describe it.

Did work contact stop? Did decision load fall? Did sensory input fall? Did you sleep more? Were meals more regular? Did someone else handle practical tasks? Did you spend time with people you enjoy? The word "rest" hides all of that.

Improvement Has an Order

Daniel's dread improved before his energy. Samir's tolerance for sound improved before his ability to manage errands. Grace's sleep improved before pleasure returned after she entered treatment.

Sequence matters because different parts of a pattern can respond at different speeds.

A low-demand weekend might show that work cues drive anxiety without restoring depleted energy. A month away from an unsustainable role may reduce cynicism while depression remains. Treatment for depression may restore interest while an unchanged workplace continues to exhaust the person.

If you record only "better" or "not better," you lose the useful part.

Activity Is Not the Opposite of Rest

Behavioral activation is an evidence-based component of depression treatment. It examines patterns of avoidance and disconnection and uses planned activity to increase contact with reinforcement and functioning. Clinical guidance treats it as a structured therapeutic approach, not a moral instruction to keep busy (Department of Veterans Affairs & Department of Defense, 2022).

This matters because the phrase "depression needs activity" is as crude as "burnout needs rest."

For a person with depression and severe sleep deprivation, more sleep may be helpful. For an autistic person with depressed mood, gentle valued activity may still be part of treatment while sensory demand is reduced. For someone with occupational burnout, exercise or social connection may support health without fixing the organizational cause.

The apparent opposition disappears once each action is specific.

Do Not Run Harmful Experiments

You do not need to prove that pushing makes you worse by pushing until you collapse.

If your function is severely reduced, use natural variations and small changes. Compare an office day with a remote day if both already occur. Compare a meeting-heavy morning with a quiet one. Notice what happens after help with errands. Notice whether an activity that usually matters gives any reward once it starts.

For treatment changes, especially medication, work with a clinician. Do not start, stop, or alter prescribed medication to test a theory from this book.

Watch for Delayed Cost

Some activities feel fine while they are happening and expensive afterward.

Autistic adults sometimes describe a delayed loss of function after sustained social or sensory demand. Workers under chronic stress may run on urgency through the week and crash on weekends. A person with depression may complete a task but experience no pleasure or sense of mastery from it.

Add a second observation point. What happens two hours later? The next morning? Does recovery time lengthen after repeated demand?

Theo could complete one client call with no obvious problem. The useful information was that after three calls he needed hours of silence and could not prepare food. The cumulative effect told more than the first call.

The Two Week Observation Window

If you are safe and not delaying needed medical care, two weeks of simple observation can give a clinician a clearer picture.

Do not change everything. Record meaningful variations that already happen. Note sleep, major work demand, social or sensory load, one measure of interest or pleasure, and one concrete function that matters to you. Add any physical symptoms or medication changes.

Two weeks is not a diagnostic threshold for burnout or autistic burnout. It simply overlaps with the minimum duration used in descriptions of depressive episodes and is long enough to capture more than one weekend (World Health Organization, 2025).

If symptoms are severe, rapidly worsening, or include safety concerns, do not wait for the observation period to end.

A Response Is Evidence About a Condition, Not Proof of a Label

Suppose you sleep for ten hours and feel better. What have you learned? That sleep mattered that night.

Suppose you take three days off and feel more interested in life. What have you learned? That a change in demand, sleep, setting, anticipation, social exposure, or several of those factors mattered.

Suppose a quieter workspace helps you finish a report. What have you learned? That the previous environment was adding a cost.

These observations are valuable. Problems begin when the conclusion jumps from "this helped" to "therefore I have X."

Many useful interventions are not specific to one diagnosis. Sleep matters across conditions. Reducing harmful overload can help almost anyone. Pleasant or meaningful activity may support people who are depressed, and it can also feel good to someone who is simply rested enough to engage. An accommodation can help an autistic person and also help a nonautistic person who concentrates better with fewer interruptions.

Use change to refine the question.

Improvement Can Have an Order

Recovery is often described as one number: better or worse. A sequence can tell you more.

Elena's work cynicism softened first. Then she stopped dreading Sunday afternoon. Physical tiredness took longer. Her interest in friends had never disappeared. That order kept work high on the list of causes.

Nora's energy improved after her sleep stabilized, but pleasure and hopelessness did not. That did not mean the sleep work failed. It showed that one symptom had changed while the broader depressive picture still needed treatment.

Samir's speech became more available before his tolerance for crowded places returned. An accommodation changed one demand but not the whole pattern.

Write down what returns first. "Energy before interest" is different from "interest was always there but access improves as demand falls."

Rest Has Several Meanings

"Rest" can mean sleep, lying down, time away from paid work, reduced sensory input, fewer decisions, solitude, social support, enjoyable activity, or simply being free from urgency. Those are not interchangeable.

A person who takes a week off work and spends it caring for a sick relative has had leave, not necessarily reduced demand. An autistic person who attends a packed family holiday may be away from the office while experiencing more sensory and social load. A depressed person may spend long periods inactive without experiencing restoration.

When someone tells you to "rest and see," ask what kind of load is actually being removed.

A more useful plan might be, "For two evenings I will remove nonessential conversation and errands," or, "For one week I will not work after 6 p.m.," or, "I will keep one planned activity that normally matters to me while reducing the work demand."

Activity Is Not a Punishment for Depression

Behavioral activation is an evidence-based psychological treatment used for depression. It focuses on links between behavior, avoidance, and mood, and uses planned activities in a structured treatment approach (Department of Veterans Affairs & Department of Defense, 2022; World Health Organization, 2025).

That is not the same as telling an exhausted person to push through every signal. It is not proof that rest is bad for depression. Sleep and recovery still matter. The clinical logic is to reduce patterns of withdrawal and inactivity that can maintain depression while selecting manageable, meaningful activity.

The distinction matters because the phrase "rest entrenches depression" is too blunt. Unstructured withdrawal can become part of a depressive cycle, but treatment decisions depend on the person, severity, safety, and clinical assessment.

The right contrast is not rest versus effort. It is intervention matched to the problem.

Do Not Conduct High-Risk Experiments

Do not stop prescribed medication to see whether your mood changes. Do not deliberately deprive yourself of sleep. Do not force overwhelming sensory exposure to prove whether you are autistic. Do not stay in a dangerous workplace to collect better data. Do not isolate yourself to see whether depression gets worse.

Observation is useful when the change is low-risk and already reasonable. Medical treatment changes belong with the appropriate clinician.

If your symptoms are severe or your safety is uncertain, the "experiment" is assessment and support, not more self-testing.

Delayed Cost Can Reverse the First Impression

Grace leaves a social event feeling energized and concludes that social contact restores her. The next day she cannot tolerate speech and misses work. Which result counts?

Both.

Some activities have an immediate emotional benefit and a delayed capacity cost. That pattern can be especially important when assessing cumulative sensory and social demand. It can also occur after demanding work, travel, or exercise for many reasons.

Record the delayed effect when it is reliable. "The meeting goes fine, but I lose the evening afterward" is a clearer statement than "meetings are fine."

A Two-Week Observation Window

Two weeks is long enough to observe some repeated patterns and short enough to avoid turning tracking into a lifestyle. It also matches the minimum duration described for a depressive episode, although only a clinician can diagnose depression and duration is only one part of the criteria (World Health Organization, 2025).

Choose three variables:

1. A demand you suspect matters.
2. A capacity marker that has changed.
3. A broad mood or interest marker.

Then record context, capacity, and change in a sentence or two each day.

At the end, do not calculate a diagnosis. Ask what you can now say more precisely.

"The office predicts the worst days, but low mood also persists on leave."

"Quiet days restore speech but not energy."

"I still want my hobbies, but I can only access them after low-demand days."

"My loss of interest is present regardless of work."

Those are useful outputs. They are the kind of observations that can shorten the distance between "I feel awful" and a clinically useful conversation.

Principles to Remember

Change gives you clues, not verdicts.

Describe what changed in the environment before judging what changed in you. Track sequence and delayed cost. Treat rest as a group of specific conditions, not a magical substance. Treat activity as something that can be structured and dosed, not as proof of willpower.

Most of all, do not make yourself earn help by performing a perfect self-experiment. The purpose of observation is to communicate more clearly, not to solve the case without a clinician.

Chapter 9: When Two Things Are True

Aisha's new job was objectively better.

The hours were shorter. Her manager was calm. She worked from home three days a week. The role removed nearly every workplace feature she had blamed for her collapse.

She was still depressed.

The change reduced one layer of strain. It did not restore pleasure, appetite, sleep, or hope. That was not evidence that the job change had failed. It was evidence that the old job had not been the whole story.

Overlap is not an annoying exception to differential thinking. It is one of the main reasons to do it well.

Chapter principle: The choice is often not "burnout or depression." Occupational burnout, depression, autistic burnout, physical illness, grief, anxiety, and other stress-related problems can overlap. A useful plan identifies which layer needs attention now instead of forcing one label to explain everything.

Research Does Not Give a Clean Wall

Burnout and depression are strongly related in the research literature. The degree to which they should be considered distinct has been debated for years.

Bianchi and colleagues reviewed 92 studies and argued that the distinction is conceptually and empirically uncertain. Koutsimani and colleagues later found significant relationships but concluded that the evidence supported treating burnout and depression as related rather than identical constructs. These are not mutually exclusive facts: high overlap can coexist with meaningful distinctions in context or measurement (Bianchi et al., 2015; Koutsimani et al., 2019).

For a reader, the practical lesson is to avoid categorical slogans.

Work Stress Can Contribute to Depression

WHO describes depression as arising from a complex interaction of social, psychological, and biological factors. Adverse life events, including unemployment and other stressors, can increase risk, while depression itself can worsen stress and functioning (World Health Organization, 2025).

A chronically hostile or overwhelming job can therefore be part of the story without being the whole diagnosis.

Marcus spent months becoming cynical, exhausted, and ineffective at work. Later he stopped enjoying family dinners and weekend cycling. His self-criticism became global. A clinician did not need to decide that the job was irrelevant in order to assess him for depression. Both levels could be true.

Autistic People Can Be Depressed Too

Autistic burnout should never be used as a reason to ignore depression.

An autistic person may experience reduced skills, sensory tolerance, and capacity from sustained demand while also developing persistent low mood, anhedonia, hopelessness, or suicidal thinking. The newer autistic burnout literature does not erase established mental health assessment.

This is especially important when someone says, "Depression treatment didn't fix my burnout, so I was never depressed." Treatment response is not a perfect retrospective diagnostic test. A person can have more than one problem, an incomplete response, side effects, the wrong treatment fit, or environmental stress that continues after mood improves.

Mixed Patterns Need Layered Plans

Think in layers rather than winners.

Layer one may be immediate safety. Layer two may be medical evaluation for fatigue or physical symptoms. Layer three may be depression treatment. Layer four may be workplace change. Layer five may be autistic accommodations and reduction of cumulative demand.

The order depends on severity and circumstances.

Nora needed a depression assessment before making a dramatic career decision because her hopelessness and loss of pleasure were broad. Ben needed to confront a role that had doubled without resources. Samir needed major demand reduction and a conversation about autistic burnout while his clinician also screened for depression.

No single layer invalidated the others.

Look for Residual Symptoms

One of the best clues to overlap appears after something improves.

Suppose time away from work removes Sunday dread and cynicism, but sleep remains disrupted and nothing feels enjoyable. That residual pattern deserves attention.

Suppose depression treatment restores interest and reduces hopelessness, but fluorescent lights, spontaneous meetings, and basic errands still produce severe functional cost. Autistic demand may still need to be addressed.

Suppose accommodations reduce sensory strain but physical exhaustion, dizziness, and breathlessness remain. That is a reason to return to medical evaluation.

Ask, "What is left after the obvious layer changes?"

Do Not Use One Label to Cancel Another

People sometimes protect a preferred explanation.

A burnout label can feel less stigmatizing than depression. An autism explanation can finally make years of experience coherent. A depression diagnosis can provide access to treatment that helped before. Each can become emotionally important.

Try not to make the label defend itself.

If new evidence does not fit, the explanation should widen. You do not lose anything by saying, "Work clearly contributed, and I may also be depressed." You do not betray an autistic understanding by asking whether a depressive episode is present. You do not minimize depression by insisting that a toxic workload still needs to change.

A Layered Sentence for Clinicians

Use one sentence that leaves room for overlap.

"I think work stress is a major part of this because ___, but the symptoms that concern me outside work are ___."

Or: "I am autistic and the loss of function and sensory tolerance feels like descriptions of autistic burnout, but I also want to be assessed for depression because ___."

Or: "I have been calling this depression, but some symptoms track work so closely that I want to discuss whether occupational burnout is contributing."

That language invites assessment instead of presenting the clinician with a conclusion they must either endorse or reject.

Overlap Is Expected, Not an Error

The research literature does not give burnout and depression a perfectly clean wall. A systematic review and meta-analysis found a substantial association between burnout and depression while concluding that the available evidence did not establish that they were the same construct (Koutsimani et al., 2019). A separate review has argued that the overlap is considerable and that the conceptual boundary deserves close scrutiny (Bianchi et al., 2015).

For a reader, the practical lesson is simple: symptoms can cluster across categories, and a good assessment should not force the story into one box too early.

Aisha's work stress was real. Her depressive symptoms were real. Treating one did not invalidate the other.

Causes and Conditions Can Stack

People often ask which thing came first because they hope the first cause will identify the diagnosis. Sometimes it helps. Sometimes the sequence is layered.

A difficult job can reduce sleep and increase isolation. Those changes can worsen mood. Depression can reduce concentration and energy, which makes work harder. A person may then work longer to compensate, increasing occupational strain. An autistic employee may mask heavily at work, arrive home with little capacity, withdraw from relationships, and later develop depression as well.

The loop does not tell you which label is "primary." It tells you which links can be addressed.

Map the sequence with arrows in plain words:

"Staff shortage -> longer hours -> stopped exercising -> sleep worsened -> concentration fell -> work took longer."

Or:

"More office days -> more sensory load -> less speech after work -> social plans canceled -> loneliness increased -> mood fell."

You are not proving causation. You are identifying plausible points for assessment and change.

Residual Symptoms Are a Useful Signal

When one part of the environment changes, watch what remains.

Marcus moved to a team with a reasonable workload. His work dread improved. His conviction that he was worthless did not. He still woke early, had little appetite, and could not enjoy weekends. The remaining symptoms strengthened the case for depression assessment.

Grace received remote-work accommodations. She regained enough capacity to cook and speak after work, but low mood and loss of interest continued. The accommodation was valuable and incomplete.

Samir began treatment for depression and his hopelessness lifted. He still had a pronounced increase in sensory sensitivity and loss of capacity after clustered social demand. The treatment response did not make that residual pattern imaginary.

Residual symptoms prevent an all-or-nothing interpretation of partial improvement.

Mixed Patterns Need Mixed Plans

If two processes are plausible, build a plan with more than one lane.

For occupational strain, that may mean reducing excessive workload, clarifying role expectations, using leave, asking for support, or considering a role change.

For depression, it may mean professional assessment and evidence-based psychological treatment, medication when appropriate, or both (World Health Organization, 2025; National Institute for Health and Care Excellence, 2022).

For autistic burnout, based on current research and community-informed descriptions, it may mean reducing cumulative demands, increasing support, and accommodating sensory, social, and executive needs while keeping other causes under review (Raymaker et al., 2020; Mantzalas et al., 2022, 2024).

The plan should not become three full-time jobs. Choose the smallest set of actions that addresses the highest-risk and highest-cost parts first.

Do Not Make Treatment Response a Retrospective Diagnosis

People sometimes reason backward: "The antidepressant helped, so it was depression," or, "Leave helped, so it was burnout."

A treatment response can support a clinical interpretation, but it rarely proves that only one thing was present. Nonspecific effects, natural change over time, improved sleep, supportive contact, reduced demand, and simultaneous interventions can all influence how someone feels.

The same caution applies when something does not help. One medication not helping does not rule out depression. One vacation not helping does not rule out work burnout. One accommodation not helping does not rule out autism or autistic burnout.

Use treatment response as one part of an ongoing assessment with the relevant professional.

The Layered Handoff

When you suspect more than one process, do not try to persuade the clinician with a long theory. Give them the layers.

"Work layer: I became exhausted and cynical during nine months of understaffing, and the dread improves when I am away."

"Whole-life layer: for the past two months I have also lost interest in hobbies, wake early, and feel hopeless even on leave."

"Capacity layer: I have a new loss of tolerance for noise and conversation that remains after the workday."

Then ask, "Could we assess depression and medical causes while also considering the work and autistic-burnout patterns?"

That is a much easier clinical question to work with than "Which one is it?"

When One Label Starts Erasing Evidence

A label becomes risky when it makes contrary evidence disappear.

"If it is burnout, of course I feel bad on weekends because I am still recovering."

"If it is depression, of course the office is the worst place because depression makes work harder."

"If it is autistic burnout, of course I do not want to socialize because I am overloaded."

Each explanation could be true. Each can also become unfalsifiable if every possible observation is used to protect it.

Keep one column titled "Does not fit my current theory." Put contradictory details there. If the column grows, bring it to the clinician. Good differential thinking becomes stronger when it can survive evidence it did not expect.

In a Nutshell

Overlap is not a failure of the Three Question Check. It is often the result.

The research relationship between burnout and depression is strong and contested. Autistic burnout adds another developing concept that can coexist with depression or job-related strain. Physical causes can sit beside all of them.

A layered explanation gives you more options than a single winner. Treat the most urgent layer first, then reassess what remains.

Chapter 10: Rule Out the Physical

By the time Luis booked an appointment, he had already decided what the doctor would say.

Stress. Sleep more. Exercise. Try not to think about work.

Instead, the doctor asked about breathlessness. Luis mentioned it almost as an afterthought. He had assumed being winded on the stairs was part of being exhausted. The conversation moved from a mental health label to a broader medical assessment.

That is the point of this chapter. Fatigue is common and nonspecific. Depression, chronic stress, and autistic burnout can all be real while a physical condition also deserves attention.

Chapter principle: Persistent or unexplained exhaustion belongs in a medical conversation, especially when it is new, severe, worsening, accompanied by physical changes, or difficult to explain from context alone. A differential that starts and ends with psychology is incomplete.

Fatigue Has Many Causes

MedlinePlus lists possible causes of fatigue that include anemia or iron deficiency, sleep disorders, thyroid disorders, medicines, persistent pain, depression, and substance use. Its material on differential diagnosis uses fatigue as an example of a symptom that can arise from many different conditions (MedlinePlus, 2025, 2026).

That list is not a home checklist for ordering your own tests. It is a reminder that a clinician needs the wider picture.

NIMH makes a similar point in its depression information: some medications and medical conditions can produce symptoms that resemble depression, and a health professional may use an interview, physical examination, and laboratory tests when appropriate to rule out other causes (National Institute of Mental Health, n.d.).

Bring the Body Into the Story

When people become convinced they are "burned out," they can stop noticing physical information.

Write down new or changed symptoms even if they seem unrelated: sleep quality, snoring, menstrual changes, appetite, weight, pain, bowel changes, fever, dizziness, breathlessness, heart racing, weakness, headaches, medication changes, or substance use. Do not try to interpret all of them. Let the clinician decide what matters.

The absence of dramatic physical symptoms does not prove the problem is psychological. The presence of a symptom does not prove a disease. The value is completeness.

Sleep Deserves More Than a Footnote

Poor sleep can be a symptom, a contributor, or both.

Work stress can keep a person alert long after the laptop closes. Depression can involve insomnia or sleeping much more than usual. Sensory or routine disruption can affect autistic people differently. Sleep disorders such as obstructive sleep apnea can also produce substantial daytime fatigue.

If you sleep for eight hours but wake unrefreshed every day, say that. If someone reports loud snoring, gasping, or pauses in breathing, mention it. If your schedule regularly allows only five hours, that matters too.

"Exhausted despite enough opportunity to sleep" and "exhausted because I am sleeping five hours" are different starting points.

Medication and Substance Changes Matter

Many prescribed and nonprescribed substances can affect sleep, energy, concentration, appetite, or mood.

The useful action is not to stop medication on your own. It is to give the prescriber an accurate list and timeline. Note when a medication started, stopped, or changed dose. Include supplements, alcohol, cannabis, stimulants, and other substances if relevant. A clinician cannot assess a factor that remains invisible.

If you suspect a medication is contributing, ask the prescriber how to evaluate that safely.

Know When Not to Wait

Some symptoms need timely or urgent medical attention regardless of your theory about burnout.

A sudden severe change, fainting, chest pain, severe shortness of breath, new neurologic symptoms, inability to keep fluids down, or other acute concerns should be assessed through appropriate urgent or emergency services. This book cannot give a complete emergency symptom list.

Mental health urgency works the same way. Thoughts of suicide, inability to maintain safety, or rapidly worsening psychiatric symptoms should move the timeline forward. In the United States, 988 provides crisis support by call or text around the clock (Substance Abuse and Mental Health Services Administration, 2025).

Prepare for the Appointment

A primary care visit can be short. Bring the information that changes the conversation.

Start with duration: "This has been going on for four months and is getting worse."

Add impact: "I am missing work, no longer cooking, and sleeping ten hours without feeling restored."

Add context: "Work makes it worse, but it is present on weekends too."

Add physical changes: "I am also getting dizzy when I stand and my periods have become heavier."

Add mental health changes: "I have lost interest in things I usually enjoy."

Then ask directly: "Could we consider both mental health and physical causes of this fatigue?"

That is not telling a doctor which tests to order. It is making sure the differential is not narrowed before the conversation begins.

Exhaustion Deserves a Broad Door

Fatigue is common and nonspecific. MedlinePlus lists many possible causes, including sleep problems, anemia, thyroid disorders, infection, chronic disease, medications, and mental health conditions, among others (MedlinePlus, 2025). The purpose of knowing this is not to scare yourself with a list. It is to remember that "I am tired because I am stressed" is a hypothesis, not a medical clearance.

NIMH similarly notes that certain medications and medical conditions, including thyroid disorders and viral illnesses, can produce symptoms that resemble depression, and that a provider may use history, examination, and laboratory tests as appropriate to rule out alternatives (National Institute of Mental Health, n.d.).

You do not need to know which test to request. You need to tell the clinician what changed.

Bring Symptoms That Do Not Fit the Story

Luis nearly omitted breathlessness because it did not fit his burnout theory. That was exactly the detail worth mentioning.

Other details that deserve to be brought into an appointment include significant change in weight or appetite, new pain, dizziness, fever, palpitations, shortness of breath, fainting, unusual bleeding, neurological symptoms, a major change in sleep, or any other new physical symptom that concerns you. The meaning depends on context and requires clinical judgment.

Do not wait for the symptom to become dramatic enough to "count." Say, "This is new for me," and describe onset and pattern.

The clinician may decide it is related to stress. The point is to let that decision happen after the physical information is visible.

Sleep Can Mimic and Magnify

Sleep deserves specific questions because poor sleep can produce fatigue, concentration problems, irritability, and reduced functioning. Depression can also disturb sleep. Work schedules can disrupt sleep. Sensory or anxiety-related factors can interfere with it. The relationship can run in more than one direction.

Instead of saying "my sleep is bad," record the type of change.

Do you struggle to fall asleep? Wake repeatedly? Wake much earlier than intended? Sleep far longer than usual? Feel unrefreshed despite enough time in bed? Snore loudly or wake gasping according to someone else? Has shift work or overtime changed your schedule?

A clinician can use those details to decide what deserves further assessment.

Medication and Substance Timing Matters

A new prescription, dose change, over-the-counter product, alcohol pattern, stimulant use, cannabis use, or change in caffeine can alter sleep, energy, mood, concentration, or appetite. The relevant effect varies by substance and person.

Do not stop prescribed medication on your own to test a theory. Bring a current medication and supplement list, including changes and dates, to the appointment. NIMH advises discussing medication benefits, side effects, and concerns with a health care provider and cautions against stopping prescribed psychiatric medication without professional guidance (National Institute of Mental Health, n.d.).

Timing can be especially helpful. "The fatigue started three weeks after the dose changed" is information. It is not proof of causation.

A Primary Care Visit Can Advance the Mental Health Question

Some readers worry that seeing a primary care clinician means their problem will be reduced to blood tests. Others worry that seeing a therapist first means a physical cause will be missed. In practice, the right route depends on access, severity, symptoms, and local systems.

If fatigue, sleep change, appetite change, concentration problems, or other physical symptoms are prominent, primary care can be a useful entry point. A clinician can review history, medications, physical symptoms, mental health symptoms, and decide what examination or testing is appropriate.

You can still say, "I am also concerned about depression," or, "The change is strongly tied to work," or, "I am autistic and my sensory tolerance and skills have changed." A broad medical assessment and a precise psychological description are not competing approaches.

Prepare Four Appointment Facts

Before the visit, write four short lines:

Onset: "This became noticeably different around ______."

Spread: "It affects ______, but ______ is relatively preserved."

Body: "The physical changes I have noticed are ______."

Safety: "I do / do not have thoughts about death, suicide, or being unable to keep myself safe."

If the safety line is positive or uncertain, do not hide it to keep the appointment simple. It changes clinical priority.

Bring a medication list and relevant diagnoses if you have them. You do not need a perfect symptom diary.

Know the Urgent Route

Some presentations should not wait for a routine differential exercise. Immediate danger, severe breathing difficulty, chest pain, new neurological symptoms, severe confusion, inability to maintain basic hydration or nutrition, or concern that you may act on suicidal thoughts can require urgent or emergency assessment depending on the situation.

This book cannot determine urgency for an individual. When in doubt about a serious or rapidly worsening physical symptom, use local urgent medical guidance or emergency services. For suicidal crisis in the United States, call or text 988; in immediate danger use emergency services (Substance Abuse and Mental Health Services Administration, 2025).

The central rule is simple: do not make the burnout-versus-depression question carry more weight than safety.

Principles to Remember

Exhaustion is real before its cause is known.

A mental health explanation does not rule out physical illness, and a physical condition does not make work stress or depression irrelevant. Persistent fatigue deserves a broad assessment when severity, duration, physical symptoms, or functional loss make that appropriate.

Bring a timeline, not a verdict. The job of the appointment is to widen the evidence before anyone narrows the answer.

Chapter 11: If Work Is Driving It

Three vacant roles sat behind the exhaustion. None of them could be solved by a better morning routine.

For nine months, Ben had treated a structural work problem as a personal capacity problem. He worked earlier, blocked his calendar, meal-prepped on Sundays, turned off notifications, and listened to podcasts about resilience while walking to meetings he no longer believed in.

The changes made him more organized. They did not change the fact that his job now contained the work of three people.

Chapter principle: If the pattern is strongly occupational, recovery requires attention to the job as well as the worker. Personal habits can support health, but they cannot reliably compensate for chronic demands that remain unreasonable, unsafe, or incompatible with available resources.

Name the Work Mechanism

"Work is stressful" is too broad to act on.

What exactly is happening? Is the workload too high? Is there low control over how work is done? Are priorities contradictory? Is staffing inadequate? Is the role morally distressing? Is there bullying or harassment? Is the schedule incompatible with sleep or caregiving? Are sensory demands unusually high? Is the job requiring constant social performance or masking?

A specific mechanism points toward a specific conversation.

Elena's main problem was not volume. It was unpredictability. Every planned task could be displaced by a senior leader's "urgent" request. Once she named that, the first experiment was not working fewer hours. It was creating a rule for who could reorder priorities and how.

Reduce Demand Where It Is Real

A useful work change removes or reshapes demand instead of adding another task to the employee's recovery plan.

That can mean workload reduction, clearer priorities, protected focus time, fewer meetings, schedule changes, additional staff, leave, remote work where appropriate, quieter space, role redesign, or a formal accommodation process. Which options are available depends on the job, country, disability status, employer, and circumstances.

This book does not give employment-law advice. If rights or formal accommodations are involved, use current local guidance or qualified advice.

What matters here is the direction: if the job is part of the problem, the job belongs in the plan.

Recovery Is Not a Weekend Project

After long periods of strain, people often expect the body to obey the calendar.

They take Friday off and become angry when Sunday still feels flat. Then they conclude the break "didn't work" and return to the same pace.

A longer recovery curve does not prove or disprove occupational burnout. It may reflect accumulated sleep loss, depression, autistic burnout, physical illness, or simple depth of exhaustion. Use the time to observe what changes rather than to demand a deadline.

Daniel's energy lagged behind his interest. That sequence was encouraging without being a promise.

Do Not Romanticize Quitting

Leaving a job can be the right choice. It can also create financial, identity, insurance, immigration, family, or career stress.

A book that tells every burned-out reader to resign is not offering serious help.

Ask whether meaningful change is possible inside the role. Ask what has already been tried. Ask whether leave creates information or simply postpones the same conditions. Ask what financial runway exists. If you are depressed, consider whether a major decision can be discussed with someone who understands both your mental health and practical circumstances.

Sometimes the answer is still to leave. The point is to make that a decision, not a reflex.

Watch What Remains After Work Changes

This is where Chapter 9 pays off.

Suppose your workload falls and Sunday dread improves, but you remain unable to enjoy anything. Suppose cynicism fades after changing teams, but you still sleep fourteen hours and feel physically ill. Suppose a quieter workspace helps concentration but speech and sensory tolerance remain sharply reduced across life.

Those residual symptoms deserve their own explanation.

Do not let a successful work intervention become evidence that every other concern was "just burnout." Improvement can reveal the next layer.

A Work Conversation Script

If you decide to ask for change, lead with function and work conditions rather than a diagnosis you may not have.

Try: "Over the last two months, the combination of three weekly deadlines and unplanned same-day requests has made it difficult to complete core work reliably. I want to discuss which priorities can be removed, delayed, or reassigned."

If sensory demand is central: "I am having difficulty maintaining concentration in the open office. I would like to discuss whether quieter workspace or more remote days are possible."

If leave is being considered, ask what will be different when you return. Leave without a change in the underlying condition can become an intermission rather than a solution.

Work Problems Need Work-Sized Changes

If the pattern is strongly occupational, the first intervention should not automatically be a new personal habit. Ask what would reduce the work mechanism itself.

If workload is the problem, a work-sized change alters volume, deadlines, staffing, or priorities. If lack of control is the problem, a work-sized change increases decision authority or predictability. If role ambiguity is the problem, it clarifies what belongs to you. If sensory demand is part of the problem, the change may involve location, equipment, scheduling, or communication format.

Some changes require a manager. Some require occupational health, human resources, a union, a disability accommodation process, or medical leave. Some are unavailable in a particular workplace.

Do not confuse "I can think of a solution" with "I have the power to implement it."

Make the Request Observable

"Please make my job less stressful" is understandable but hard to act on.

A more observable request sounds like:

"For the next four weeks, can we reduce my active projects from eight to five and agree which three are paused?"

"Can we set a rule that urgent requests come through one channel rather than four?"

"Can I receive agendas before client calls and use written follow-up for complex questions?"

"Can we review which responsibilities belong to the vacant role rather than assuming they remain with me?"

The request does not need to explain your entire mental health history. It needs to identify the demand and the proposed change.

Boundaries Need Consequences in the System

Ben had told his manager he could not sustain the workload. The manager agreed sympathetically and assigned three more tasks the next week. Ben interpreted the failed conversation as evidence that he had communicated badly.

Sometimes the system understood perfectly and did not change.

A boundary that depends entirely on someone else's goodwill may not protect capacity. The next step may be escalation, documentation, leave, external advice, a transfer, or planning an exit. The right choice depends on resources and risk.

This is where burnout books can become unfair. "Set boundaries" sounds simple when the reader bears all the financial consequences of enforcing them. A useful plan includes what you can control and what you cannot.

Leave Can Be Treatment for Demand, Not a Verdict on the Career

Time away can serve several purposes: interrupting acute overload, creating space for medical or mental health assessment, restoring sleep, reducing exposure to a harmful environment, or giving enough capacity to make decisions.

It does not answer whether you should quit. It also does not guarantee recovery.

Use leave, where available and clinically appropriate, as time to gather information. Which symptoms change? Which do not? What returns first? What happens to work dread when the work is absent? Are low mood and loss of interest still broad? Do sensory and communication difficulties remain?

A return-to-work plan should be based on the pattern you learned, not only on the calendar.

Do Not Use Productivity as the Recovery Metric

A burned-out worker often wants proof of recovery in the form of output. "I cleared my inbox, so I am better." That can restart the same cycle.

Choose measures that reflect sustainability: less anticipatory dread, ability to stop work at the planned time, recovery that no longer consumes every evening, restored interest outside work, improved sleep, or a return of professional confidence.

If productivity rises because you are again working at night, that is not evidence the underlying work pattern improved.

Quitting Is a Decision, Not a Treatment

For some people, leaving is the right move. For others, it is financially dangerous, unnecessary, or impossible. A new job can remove the current stressor but preserve a pattern of overwork, lack of support, sensory overload, or depression.

Before resigning, when circumstances allow, ask:

What specific conditions am I leaving?

Which of those conditions are likely to change elsewhere?

What symptoms do I expect to improve if work is the main driver?

What will I do if the whole-life symptoms remain?

This protects the job decision from carrying the full burden of a mental health diagnosis.

A Four-Week Work Test

If your situation is safe enough and you have some ability to alter demand, choose one meaningful work change for four weeks. It should be large enough to matter and specific enough to describe.

Examples include reducing overtime, working from home on fixed days, removing one recurring low-value responsibility, stopping after-hours email, moving out of a noisy workspace, or receiving written priorities.

Track one occupational marker and one whole-life marker.

Occupational marker: dread, cynicism, professional confidence, recovery after the workday.

Whole-life marker: interest in a hobby, connection, sleep, appetite, broad low mood.

If work markers improve and whole-life markers were relatively intact, the occupational explanation gains weight. If whole-life symptoms remain significant, bring that residual pattern to a clinician.

Again, this is not a diagnostic test. It is a way to learn whether changing the suspected demand changes the problem.

The Conversation After No Change

Sometimes you make a reasonable work change and nothing improves.

Do not immediately conclude that the change was too small or that you failed to rest correctly. Ask whether the hypothesis needs widening.

"Reducing meetings helped my sensory load but not the hopelessness."

"Three weeks of leave reduced exhaustion but I still cannot enjoy anything."

"The new manager is supportive, yet I am still waking early and struggling to eat."

Those are strong reasons to revisit depression and medical causes, not reasons to double down on burnout language.

In a Nutshell

When work is the main driver, make work visible.

Identify the demand, not only the feeling. Look for changes that remove load, increase control, or improve fit. Use rest as recovery, not as a test you must pass on schedule. Avoid making irreversible career decisions from a slogan.

And keep checking the wider pattern. Occupational burnout can be real while depression, autistic burnout, or physical illness is also present.

Chapter 12: If Depression Is Present

Nora's first goal in treatment was surprisingly small.

Not "be happy." Not "get my life back." Not "return to full productivity."

It was to eat breakfast at the table three mornings that week.

The task mattered because depression treatment is not a contest between rest and effort. It is an individualized plan built around severity, safety, preferences, functioning, and evidence-based options.

Chapter principle: If depression is present or strongly suspected, move from self-differential to professional care. Evidence-based psychological treatments and medications are available, and the right plan depends on the person and the severity of the episode.

Assessment Comes Before Optimization

Depression is more than a low mood score.

A clinician may ask about duration, mood, interest or pleasure, sleep, appetite, energy, concentration, guilt, hopelessness, psychomotor changes, functioning, substance use, prior episodes, family history, medical contributors, and safety. They may also ask about periods of unusually elevated or irritable mood, reduced need for sleep, or other features that could change the diagnostic picture.

You do not need to know which questions matter most. Your job is to answer accurately.

Bring the Three Question Check notes. They give context without telling the clinician what conclusion to reach.

Treatment Is Not One Thing

WHO states that effective treatments for depression include psychological treatment and medication, with choices depending on severity and circumstances. NICE and VA/DoD guidance discuss several evidence-based psychotherapies and medication approaches for adults with depression (World Health Organization, 2025; National Institute for Health and Care Excellence, 2022; Department of Veterans Affairs & Department of Defense, 2022).

That means there is no single "depression treatment" against which you must judge yourself.

Psychotherapy approaches differ. Medications differ. Some people need combination treatment. Some need a change after an initial approach does not help enough. Severe or treatment-resistant depression may involve additional specialist options.

A poor fit with one treatment is not proof that the diagnosis is wrong.

Behavioral Activation Is Not Forced Positivity

Behavioral activation often becomes distorted online into "do things even when you don't feel like it."

The clinical approach is more thoughtful. It examines the relationship between behavior, avoidance, context, and mood, then uses planned activities to increase contact with experiences that can provide reinforcement, mastery, connection, or meaning. It is adjusted to the person's situation (Department of Veterans Affairs & Department of Defense, 2022).

For an exhausted reader, this distinction is critical.

A clinician using behavioral activation should not need you to pretend sensory overload is laziness or that an impossible workload is healthy. If you are autistic, say what particular forms of activity cost. If work is unsafe or overwhelming, say that too. Good treatment works with the real context.

Rest Can Still Belong

Depression does not make rest forbidden.

Sleep, physical recovery, nutrition, medical care, and relief from acute stress can matter to anyone. The question is whether rest is supporting recovery or becoming part of a cycle of withdrawal that deepens disconnection for that particular person.

That is an assessment question, not a moral judgment.

Grace needed more sleep after months of insomnia. She also needed small planned contact with people she trusted because isolation was worsening her mood. Both were true. The plan did not ask her to choose a camp called rest or a camp called activity.

Medication Decisions Need a Prescriber

Do not use this book to start, stop, change, or compare antidepressants.

NIMH advises working with a health professional to develop a medication plan suited to individual needs and notes that people respond differently to medications. Medication information and safety guidance change over time (National Institute of Mental Health, n.d.).

If you think a medication is not helping, is causing side effects, or may be contributing to fatigue, bring that concern to the prescriber. Abrupt changes can carry risks depending on the medication.

Measure More Than Productivity

A person can improve before work performance returns.

Track interest, hope, sleep, appetite, concentration, social connection, self-criticism, and safety as well as output. If the only outcome you monitor is how quickly you can return to full workload, you may miss recovery or pressure it into the wrong shape.

Nora's breakfasts mattered because they marked a return of routine, appetite, and contact with the day. Later goals became larger. The first useful change was small and observable.

Know the Safety Door

If suicidal thoughts are present, say so directly to a clinician. If you may act on those thoughts or cannot keep yourself safe, seek urgent help rather than waiting for the perfect appointment.

In the United States, call or text 988 for the 988 Suicide & Crisis Lifeline. In life-threatening situations, use emergency services. Outside the United States, use the crisis or emergency service where you live (Substance Abuse and Mental Health Services Administration, 2025).

Safety gets its own door. You do not need to solve the burnout question before opening it.

Start With Severity and Function

Depression treatment is not one identical package. Clinical guidelines consider factors such as symptom severity, duration, functional impact, prior treatment, preferences, coexisting conditions, and safety when choosing care (National Institute for Health and Care Excellence, 2022; Department of Veterans Affairs & Department of Defense, 2022).

That is why a book cannot tell you which treatment you need. It can help you describe what the clinician needs to know.

Nora's appointment became more useful when she stopped trying to answer "How depressed are you?" and described function: she was eating once a day, waking at 4 a.m., no longer enjoying friends, taking twice as long to complete routine work, and having recurrent thoughts that everyone would be better off without her.

Severity becomes visible through specifics.

Psychological Treatment Is Not Generic Talking

WHO lists several effective psychological treatments for depression, including behavioral activation, cognitive behavioral therapy, interpersonal psychotherapy, and problem-solving therapy (World Health Organization, 2025). Which option is available or appropriate depends on clinical context and local services.

The practical point is that "therapy" is not one method. If a previous experience felt unhelpful, tell the next clinician what approach you tried, for how long, and what did or did not change.

A useful question is, "What treatment are you recommending, what is it intended to target, and how will we know whether it is helping?"

That question turns treatment into a plan rather than a vague instruction to talk about your feelings.

Behavioral Activation Has a Specific Logic

Behavioral activation is sometimes described online as "do things even when you do not feel like it." That is incomplete.

Clinical behavioral activation is a structured approach that examines links among activity, avoidance, reinforcement, and mood, then schedules manageable activities aligned with goals and functioning (Department of Veterans Affairs & Department of Defense, 2022).

For an exhausted reader, this distinction matters. The goal is not to recreate a punishing productivity schedule. A planned ten-minute walk with a friend may be an activation target. So may eating breakfast at a table, attending a treatment appointment, or returning to one valued routine.

If activity repeatedly causes a large delayed crash or sensory overload, tell the clinician. A treatment plan needs the full capacity picture.

Medication Needs Follow-Up, Not a Verdict

Antidepressant medication is one treatment option for depression, with use depending on severity, preferences, medical factors, and clinical guidance (World Health Organization, 2025; National Institute for Health and Care Excellence, 2022).

NIMH notes that antidepressants can take several weeks to work and that some symptoms may improve before mood does (National Institute of Mental Health, n.d.). That means a few difficult days, or an early change in sleep without a mood change, should not be turned into a self-directed conclusion about whether the medication "proves" anything.

Report side effects, concerns, and changes to the prescriber. Do not stop a prescribed psychiatric medication abruptly without professional advice.

Rest Still Has a Place

The phrase "rest makes depression worse" is an unhelpful overstatement.

A depressed person still needs adequate sleep and physical recovery. Someone with depression may also be physically ill, burned out from work, caregiving, disabled, autistic, or recovering from prolonged overload. Rest can be necessary.

The clinical concern is not rest itself. It is when withdrawal and inactivity become part of a cycle that reduces contact with activities, people, or routines that support functioning and mood. Behavioral activation addresses that cycle in a planned way.

A better question is, "Which rest restores me, and which withdrawal seems to make the world smaller?" Bring that observation into treatment.

Measure More Than Work Output

Depression can improve before productivity catches up, especially if someone is returning from a period of severe impairment. It can also happen the other way around: a person may force output before mood or safety improves.

Track a few domains the treatment is actually meant to change.

Interest or pleasure: Are any activities beginning to register again?

Connection: Is contact with other people becoming more possible or meaningful?

Basic routines: Is eating or sleep becoming more regular?

Thinking: Is hopelessness or self-condemnation less dominant?

Function: Can ordinary tasks be started and completed with less effort?

Safety: Have thoughts of death or suicide changed in frequency, intensity, or urgency?

The clinician may use formal measures too. Your observations add context.

Work Can Still Need Changing

A depression diagnosis does not certify the workplace as healthy.

If the job remains chronically understaffed, abusive, unsafe, incompatible with disability needs, or otherwise unsustainable, treatment should not become a method for tolerating unlimited harm. You can work on depression and work conditions at the same time.

This is the core reason the differential is not a contest. One answer does not cancel the others.

If Safety Changes, Act on Safety

Thoughts about death and suicide can occur in depression and require direct attention. If you are in the United States and are struggling or having thoughts of suicide, call or text 988. If there is immediate danger, use emergency services. Elsewhere, use local crisis and emergency services.

Tell the clinician plainly if safety has changed. Do not soften it because you fear being dramatic, and do not wait until you have settled whether burnout also applies.

The correct next step can be urgent even when the final diagnosis is still being worked out.

Principles to Remember

If depression is in the picture, the next step is not to prove it to yourself. It is to get assessed and discuss treatment.

Treatment can include psychological approaches, medication, or combinations, depending on severity and individual circumstances. Behavioral activation is structured, not punitive. Rest is not automatically wrong. Work conditions and autistic needs still count.

A diagnosis should make the plan more accurate, not make the rest of your life disappear.

Chapter 13: If Autistic Burnout Fits

On paper, the recovery plan looked almost empty. It contained one fewer social event, a decision to treat grocery delivery as infrastructure, written agendas before meetings, ear protection on the train, and slower replies to nonurgent messages.

Samir had chosen each change because it reduced a specific demand.

None of those changes proved he had autistic burnout. They reduced identifiable demands while he and his clinicians continued assessing mood, physical health, and functioning.

Chapter principle: When autistic burnout is a plausible part of the picture, focus on reduced capacity and demand mismatch. Lowering avoidable load, increasing predictability, and using accommodations may support function, while depression and medical causes should still be assessed on their own terms.

Start With the Evidence We Have

Raymaker and colleagues described autistic burnout through autistic adults' accounts as a pattern involving chronic exhaustion, loss of skills, and reduced tolerance to stimulus. Mantzalas and colleagues later found similar themes in online material and developed research on risk, protective factors, and measurement. A 2024 study evaluated measures of autistic burnout, showing that the field is moving toward better assessment while still developing (Raymaker et al., 2020; Mantzalas et al., 2022, 2024).

This is enough to take the experience seriously.

It is not enough to claim that a particular protocol is universally proven to "treat autistic burnout." Be cautious with precise recovery formulas.

Lower Demand With Specificity

"Do less" is vague and can create guilt.

Ask which demand has the highest cost. Sensory input? Switching? Social performance? Unpredictability? Travel? Spoken communication? Planning meals? Administrative tasks? Constant availability?

Remove or support one expensive layer.

Theo moved two meetings to written updates. That freed enough capacity to cook dinner. Aisha kept meetings but moved them away from the noisiest office. Talia asked her partner to take over appointment scheduling for a month.

The goal is not permanent retreat from life. It is to stop treating every current limitation as a challenge to overcome immediately.

Accommodations Are Information

An accommodation changes the environment or task so function becomes more accessible.

If a quieter space, written instructions, predictable scheduling, communication alternatives, or help with executive tasks meaningfully changes capacity, that tells you something useful. It does not tell you that the difficulty was fake or that you should have solved it sooner.

Formal workplace accommodations depend on local law and individual circumstances. Informal supports can also matter.

If you are seeking an autism assessment, keep examples of what helps and what fails. They can show the difference between ability under ideal conditions and ability under ordinary demand.

Masking Deserves a Cost Audit

If masking or camouflaging is part of your experience, ask where it is most expensive.

Do you rehearse ordinary interactions for long periods? Monitor facial expression or eye contact constantly? Force speech when written communication would be easier? Suppress movement that helps regulate attention? Stay in painful sensory environments because leaving would look unusual?

Do not turn this into a purity test about being "more autistic." People mask for safety, employment, belonging, habit, and many other reasons. Reducing masking can have social consequences, and not every setting is safe for full disclosure.

The practical question is whether some performance demands can be reduced without creating greater harm.

Protect the Depression Differential

A dangerous mistake would be to reinterpret every depressive symptom as autistic burnout.

If interest and pleasure have broadly disappeared, hopelessness is persistent, self-worth has collapsed, or suicidal thoughts are present, ask for a depression assessment. If a clinician knows less about autistic burnout, you can bring the research term and your observations without asking them to accept a self-diagnosis.

Try: "I am autistic and I have had a marked loss of function and sensory tolerance after sustained demand. I know autistic burnout is still a developing research area. I also want to be assessed for depression and physical causes because my sleep and interest have changed."

That sentence does more work than "I know it's autistic burnout."

Recovery May Be Nonlinear

A repeated theme in autistic burnout accounts is that recovery can take time and that returning to the exact conditions that preceded collapse may recreate the problem. Qualitative research should not be converted into a guaranteed timeline.

Use function markers rather than a deadline.

Can you tolerate a little more sound? Is speech easier? Can you switch tasks without losing the rest of the day? Are familiar interests more accessible? Does one social event now require hours rather than days of recovery?

Small changes count because they are changes in capacity.

Do Not Build a Smaller Prison

Demand reduction can become so broad that life loses connection, autonomy, or support. Depression can also drive withdrawal. This is where individualized help matters.

The aim is not to eliminate every demand. It is to create enough margin that necessary and valued activities become possible again.

Samir kept one weekly visit with a friend because it mattered to him and was low demand. He dropped a larger social group that required constant conversation. The distinction was not "socializing good" or "socializing bad." It was cost, value, and current capacity.

Current Research Supports Caution and Specificity

The published autistic burnout literature has helped formalize experiences autistic people had been describing for years. Raymaker and colleagues identified chronic exhaustion, loss of skills, and reduced tolerance to stimulus as central characteristics in their qualitative work (Raymaker et al., 2020). Later research has explored online descriptions and the measurement of autistic burnout (Mantzalas et al., 2022, 2024). A 2025 systematic review synthesized 48 studies of autistic burnout and found recurring themes of debilitating exhaustion, increased disability, sensory and social overwhelm, and camouflaging (Ali et al., 2025).

The research is meaningful and still developing. That combination should shape the language you use with yourself and clinicians.

"This resembles autistic burnout" is a defensible starting point.

"This proves every symptom I have is autistic burnout" is not.

Reduce Demand by Category

"Do less" is too vague. Name the demand.

Sensory demand: noise, light, touch, smell, temperature, visual clutter, travel.

Social demand: group interaction, small talk, conflict, live conversation, unfamiliar people, being observed.

Executive demand: switching, planning, sequencing, remembering, deciding, interruptions.

Communication demand: spontaneous speech, phone calls, rapid responses, ambiguous messages.

Masking demand: monitoring expression, suppressing natural movement, rehearsing, copying social behavior, hiding distress.

Practical demand: cooking, cleaning, forms, appointments, transport, caregiving.

Choose the categories that changed most. Reducing one category tells you more than canceling every part of life.

Preserve Valued Contact Where Possible

Autistic burnout can make social contact costly. Depression can also drive withdrawal. The solution is not automatically total isolation.

Samir stopped large dinners but kept a quiet weekly visit with his brother. The change reduced sensory and conversational load without removing a relationship he valued.

Grace changed a group hobby to an online one for a period. Priya asked friends to make plans earlier instead of same-day.

The principle is demand reduction with discrimination. Remove cost where possible without assuming that every activity which requires effort is harmful.

If you notice broad loss of interest or increasing hopelessness as your world becomes smaller, bring depression back into the assessment.

Accommodations Can Be Small and Specific

An accommodation is useful when it changes the demand that is consuming capacity.

Written instructions reduce live processing. A fixed schedule reduces unpredictability. Remote work may reduce commuting and sensory exposure. Ear protection can reduce noise where safe. Grocery delivery removes travel, lighting, choice, and social steps. A prepared meal may remove sequencing and cleanup.

The effect may be modest. That still counts.

Keep the question functional: "What does this adjustment let me do that I could not do before?" If the answer is nothing, reconsider the target rather than treating the accommodation as a moral obligation.

Masking Needs a Cost Description

A broad command to "unmask" can be unsafe or impractical. People mask for many reasons, including employment, discrimination, privacy, and social expectations.

Instead of making unmasking a rule, identify costly behaviors and where there is enough safety to reduce them.

Maybe you stop forcing eye contact in one familiar meeting. Maybe you allow yourself to use a script. Maybe you decline an optional social event rather than performing through it. Maybe you use direct language with one trusted person about needing quiet.

Notice whether the change reduces exhaustion or improves access to skills. The aim is not authenticity as a performance. It is reducing unnecessary demand where you have choice.

Recovery Can Be Uneven

One week, speech is easier but errands remain impossible. Another week, you can work longer but sensory tolerance falls. A sudden busy period can cost more than expected.

Uneven improvement is frustrating because it resists a simple recovery graph. It also gives information.

Record which capacities return under which conditions. If the same accommodation repeatedly restores a particular function, that is worth sharing with a clinician or support person. If a symptom remains unchanged across reduced demand, that too deserves attention.

Depression Screening Still Matters

Autistic burnout and depression can coexist. Depression should not be dismissed as "just autism" when there is sustained low mood or loss of interest or pleasure with associated symptoms and impairment.

WHO describes depression as a pattern that can include low mood or loss of pleasure, poor concentration, guilt or low self-worth, hopelessness, sleep and appetite changes, low energy, and thoughts of death or suicide (World Health Organization, 2025).

If those features are present, ask directly for depression assessment. Autistic communication differences or a history of masking may affect how symptoms are described, so concrete examples of change from your own baseline can help.

Build a Demand Budget Without Turning Life Into Arithmetic

A "budget" here is not a points system. It is a decision rule.

Choose one nonnegotiable demand, one reducible demand, and one restorative or valued activity.

For example:

Nonnegotiable: three work shifts.

Reducible: grocery store, replaced by delivery.

Valued: quiet drawing for twenty minutes after dinner.

Then watch whether capacity becomes more stable over a week.

If you add a major demand, remove one where possible. If a routine activity begins costing far more than usual, treat that as information rather than failure.

The goal is not to make life permanently smaller. It is to stop spending capacity as if it were unchanged while you work out what is happening.

In a Nutshell

Autistic burnout is a serious, increasingly studied experience, but its research base is still developing.

Use the concept to describe sustained demand, exhaustion, loss of function, sensory changes, and the cost of masking where relevant. Reduce identifiable load and use supports without treating those changes as a diagnostic proof.

Keep other doors open. Autistic people can have depression, occupational burnout, sleep disorders, medical conditions, and ordinary life crises too.

Chapter 14: Take the Question Forward

There is a particular kind of appointment that goes badly before it begins.

You have been thinking about the problem for months. You have read hundreds of pages. You have a theory. The clinician has twenty minutes and asks, "So, what brings you in?"

Everything comes out at once.

This chapter is about making the answer shorter without making it smaller.

Chapter principle: A clinician does not need your entire internal debate. They need the timeline, the main functional changes, the cross-setting pattern, safety information, physical symptoms, relevant history, and the questions you want examined. The Three Question Check becomes useful when it can be handed off.

Lead With Function

Start with what has changed.

"I have been exhausted for four months and I am now missing work twice a week."

"I used to manage shopping and phone calls independently. Now both can take the rest of the day to recover from."

"I have lost interest in music, friends, and food, not only work."

Those statements are harder to dismiss as vague stress because they describe impairment.

Then add timing and context.

Give the Three Answers

For context, say where symptoms are strongest and whether they spread.

For capacity, name the abilities or interests that changed.

For change, describe what happens when major demands change.

A concise handoff might sound like this:

"This began after a staffing change in March. Work triggers the worst dread, but by June I had also lost interest in hobbies and was sleeping ten hours without feeling restored. Two weeks off reduced the work dread but not the loss of pleasure. I want to be assessed for depression and physical causes as well as discuss occupational burnout."

Another:

"I am autistic. After a year of high social and sensory demand, I have lost a lot of functional capacity, including speech under pressure and tolerance for grocery stores. Quiet and fewer obligations help somewhat, but recovery is slow. My mood is low too, so I want to separate autistic burnout from depression rather than assume one explanation."

Neither speech requires you to be right.

Ask Direct Questions

Good questions are specific enough to answer.

"Could depression explain the symptoms that continue outside work?"

"Are there physical causes of fatigue we should consider based on my history and symptoms?"

"I am autistic and have had a marked loss of function and sensory tolerance. How would you assess depression alongside that?"

"If we treat depression, what changes should prompt us to reconsider the role of work or autistic burnout?"

"What should I do if my symptoms worsen before the follow-up?"

These questions invite clinical reasoning.

When a Clinician Uses Different Language

Not every clinician will use "autistic burnout." Some may know the research well. Others may be unfamiliar with it or may prefer to describe the specific functional changes rather than adopt the term.

You can keep the conversation productive by returning to observable facts.

"I understand the term may not be part of your diagnostic system. The changes I want help with are loss of speech under stress, much lower sensory tolerance, and a major reduction in executive function after sustained demand."

The label can be discussed without making it the price of care.

When You Feel Dismissed

Sometimes a clinician may focus too quickly on one explanation. Sometimes the appointment is simply short and the language misses.

Ask what evidence led to the conclusion. Ask what alternatives were considered. Ask what would make them reassess. If you remain concerned, seeking a second opinion may be reasonable where access allows.

You can also bring someone you trust, request communication accommodations, or provide a brief written summary if spoken appointments are difficult.

If the issue involves urgent safety, do not wait for a better-fit routine appointment.

Make the Handoff One Page

Your final handoff can fit on one page without a table.

Use seven short headings with one or two sentences each: onset, work context, life outside work, capacity changes, mood and interest, physical and sleep changes, and what changes with reduced demand or activity.

Finish with three questions you want answered.

Do not include every article you read. If autistic burnout is important to the conversation, bringing the citation for one or two peer-reviewed papers can be enough. Raymaker et al. (2020) and Mantzalas et al. (2024) are reasonable starting points for a clinician who wants to review the concept.

The Decision After the Appointment

An assessment rarely ends every uncertainty in one visit.

You may be asked to complete screening measures, have laboratory tests, return for follow-up, try a treatment, change work conditions, or seek a specialist. Keep using the same three questions.

What changed after the intervention? Which symptoms remain? Did function improve in one setting but not another? What new evidence appeared?

Differential thinking is not a one-time puzzle. It is a process of updating the explanation when the pattern changes.

A Clinician Needs the Change, Not the Essay

You may have read enough to explain the entire history of burnout research. That is rarely the best use of a short appointment.

Lead with the change from baseline.

"Over the last three months I have become exhausted and cynical at work, and it improves noticeably after two days away."

"For eight weeks I have also lost interest in things I normally enjoy, and that does not improve on leave."

"I am autistic, and my tolerance for noise and spontaneous speech has dropped sharply since a period of heavy demand."

Those sentences contain time, scope, and function. They give the clinician places to ask follow-up questions.

Bring the Three Question Check

Your one-page handoff can have three headings.

Context: When did the change begin? Where is it strongest? What tends to precede it?

Capacity: Which abilities, interests, or tolerances changed most?

Change: What has improved or worsened with leave, reduced demand, treatment, accommodations, sleep, or other meaningful changes?

Keep each section to two or three sentences. Add a brief medication list and important physical symptoms if relevant.

The page is not a self-diagnosis form. It is a way to protect the most important information from disappearing when the appointment feels rushed.

Ask for the Differential Explicitly

You are allowed to ask what else the clinician is considering.

Useful questions include:

"Could depression explain this pattern, and what would make you more or less concerned about that?"

"Because the exhaustion is strongly work-linked, how should we think about occupational burnout alongside depression?"

"I am autistic, or I am being assessed for autism. Could the loss of skills and sensory tolerance fit autistic burnout, and what else should we rule out?"

"Are there physical or medication-related causes of fatigue that should be considered?"

You are not instructing the clinician. You are making the question visible.

If the Clinician Does Not Use the Same Term

A clinician may be familiar with occupational burnout but not autistic burnout. They may use different language for functional decline, overload, stress, or depression. That does not automatically mean the appointment failed.

Return to observations.

"Whatever term we use, the change I need help with is that speech and sensory tolerance have become much less reliable after prolonged demand."

"Whatever the label, I am losing interest across settings and waking very early."

"Whatever we call it, work cynicism and exhaustion improve when the workload is removed."

Precise function can survive disagreement about vocabulary.

If You Feel Dismissed

Sometimes a clinician has a reasonable alternative explanation. Sometimes they are working with limited time. Sometimes dismissal really happens.

Before deciding which one occurred, ask for the reasoning.

"What features make depression less likely in your view?"

"What would you want to see before investigating a physical cause?"

"What should I do if the symptoms continue after the work change?"

"Could you document that I reported this loss of function?"

If the concern remains unresolved and you have access, a second opinion may be appropriate, especially when symptoms are persistent, severe, rapidly changing, or interfering substantially with life.

A One-Page Handoff Template

Use the following as prose, not a test.

Reason for visit: "I am trying to understand a sustained change in energy, mood, and function and whether work burnout, depression, autistic burnout, a physical cause, or more than one factor could be involved."

Onset: one or two dated phases.

Context: the clearest contrast between work, home, leave, low-demand settings, or particular types of demand.

Capacity: two or three abilities or interests that changed.

Change: one or two interventions or environmental changes and what happened.

Physical and medication factors: new physical symptoms, sleep change, medication or substance changes if relevant.

Safety: whether you have thoughts of death, suicide, or concern about keeping yourself safe.

Questions: the two things you most want the clinician to assess.

That is enough.

After the Appointment, Do Not Demand Certainty Too Soon

A good first appointment may end with a plan rather than a label. The clinician may want blood tests, a follow-up, a depression measure, a medication review, more history, or referral to another professional.

Write down what is being tested and what happens next.

"Check physical contributors."

"Begin depression treatment and review in four weeks."

"Reduce work demand while monitoring whole-life symptoms."

"Discuss autism-related capacity changes with an appropriate clinician."

A staged plan is not a failure of diagnosis. Differential assessment often works by gathering evidence over time.

Know the Threshold for Faster Help

Do not wait for the next routine appointment if safety changes sharply, if you are unable to maintain basic needs, or if a serious physical symptom develops.

In the United States, call or text 988 if you are struggling or having thoughts of suicide. If you are in immediate danger, use emergency services (Substance Abuse and Mental Health Services Administration, 2025). In other countries, use local crisis or emergency services.

The purpose of this book is to make the question clearer. It should never become a reason to delay urgent help.

End With the Decision You Actually Need

Most readers do not need to leave the clinician's office able to defend a label. They need to know what to do next.

Ask for the next decision in plain language:

"What should I change now?"

"What should we monitor?"

"When should I come back?"

"What would make this urgent?"

"What other explanation are we still considering?"

That is the handoff from self-observation to professional assessment. It is also where the book's job ends.

Principles to Remember

Your goal is not to win a label. It is to get the right questions examined.

Lead with function and timing. Use context, capacity, and change to organize the story. State safety and physical symptoms directly. Ask what alternatives were considered and what would trigger reassessment.

The handoff is the final purpose of the Three Question Check: clearer observations, shorter explanations, and a better clinical conversation.

Conclusion: A Better Question Is Progress

The promise of a book with "burnout or depression" in the title can easily become dishonest.

The dishonest version gives you a quiz, adds up the answers, and sends you away with a label. It feels satisfying because uncertainty disappears. It is also exactly the kind of certainty this subject does not support.

Occupational burnout has a useful formal boundary: WHO defines it around chronic workplace stress and the occupational context. Depression is a mental disorder with a broader symptom pattern that can include persistent low mood, loss of interest or pleasure, sleep and appetite changes, concentration problems, low energy, guilt, hopelessness, and suicidal thinking. Autistic burnout has an emerging peer-reviewed literature centered on sustained demand, exhaustion, reduced function, and lower tolerance for stimulus. The boundaries between lived experiences are not perfectly clean (World Health Organization, 2019, 2025; Raymaker et al., 2020; Koutsimani et al., 2019).

That is why the Three Question Check never became a score.

Context asks where the pattern lives. Capacity asks what has become unavailable. Change asks what shifts when demands, supports, activity, setting, or treatment change. Together they create a description that can survive contact with someone who does not share your preferred explanation.

The most useful outcome may be a sentence with "and" in it.

"Work is a major driver, and I have symptoms outside work that need a depression assessment."

"I am autistic and my functional loss fits the developing research on autistic burnout, and I also need physical causes of fatigue ruled out."

"My depression is improving, and the job is still unsustainable."

Those are not weak answers. They are more accurate than forcing a complicated life into a binary.

If you have reached the end of this book, take the one-page clinician handoff from Chapter 14 and finish it. Do not wait until the wording is elegant. Put down the onset, the settings, the functions that changed, what happened to interest and pleasure, sleep and physical symptoms, what changes when demand changes, and the questions you want examined.

Then decide where the handoff belongs.

If the pattern is persistent, broad, severe, medically unexplained, or accompanied by major loss of function, a health professional is a reasonable next stop. If thoughts of suicide or immediate safety concerns are present, use urgent support. If the work connection is strong, the workplace still belongs in the plan. If autistic demand and loss of capacity are central, bring those observations too.

You do not need to know the answer before you ask for help.

The question has done its job when it gets you to a better next step.

About the Decoding the Overlap Series

Decoding the Overlap is for the questions that come before the diagnosis.

Some of the most consequential questions in mental health and neurodivergence come down to telling apart experiences that can look almost identical from the inside. Is this OCD or autism? A meltdown or a panic attack? Burnout or depression? ADHD or something closer to bipolar?

The distinctions matter because different problems call for different assessment and treatment decisions. Yet many books begin after the question is settled. This series begins before it.

Most volumes place two commonly confused conditions side by side. This volume adds autistic burnout as a third pattern because the everyday word "burnout" can cover more than one experience. Leaving that pattern out would make the comparison less useful for autistic readers and for people still being assessed.

Each volume explains what the candidate conditions are, what differences a reader can observe without diagnosing themselves, why one intervention should not be used as a home test for another condition, and what to say to a clinician to get the question properly examined.

These books do not diagnose. No book can. They offer a clearer picture of what you might be looking at and the language to take to someone who can help.

About the Author

Evie Dove Huynh writes plain-language guides for people caught between two possible explanations for what they're experiencing.

Her books grew out of a simple observation: most self-help assumes you already know what you're dealing with. The shelves are full of books about OCD, about autism, about burnout, and almost nothing for the person still trying to work out which one applies to them. That gap is where people lose years.

She writes for the reader in that gap. Every book draws on current peer-reviewed research, cites its sources so you can check them, and explains the distinctions in language you could repeat to a doctor. She doesn't diagnose, and she's clear about that throughout. What she offers is the vocabulary and the questions to take to someone who can.

Evie writes full-time and reads more clinical literature than is strictly healthy.

References

Ali, D., Bougoure, M., Cooper, B., Quinton, A. M. G., Tan, D., Brett, J., Mandy, W., Maybery, M., Magiati, I., & Happé, F. (2025). Burnout as experienced by autistic people: A systematic review. Clinical Psychology Review, 122, Article 102669. https://doi.org/10.1016/j.cpr.2025.102669

Bianchi, R., Schonfeld, I. S., & Laurent, E. (2015). Burnout-depression overlap: A review. Clinical Psychology Review, 36, 28-41. https://doi.org/10.1016/j.cpr.2015.01.004

Department of Veterans Affairs, & Department of Defense. (2022). VA/DoD clinical practice guideline for the management of major depressive disorder (Version 4.0). https://www.healthquality.va.gov/guidelines/MH/mdd/

Koutsimani, P., Montgomery, A., & Georganta, K. (2019). The relationship between burnout, depression, and anxiety: A systematic review and meta-analysis. Frontiers in Psychology, 10, 284. https://doi.org/10.3389/fpsyg.2019.00284

Mantzalas, J., Richdale, A. L., Adikari, A., Lowe, J., & Dissanayake, C. (2022). What is autistic burnout? A thematic analysis of posts on two online platforms. Autism in Adulthood, 4(1), 52-65. https://doi.org/10.1089/aut.2021.0021

Mantzalas, J., Richdale, A. L., Li, X., & Dissanayake, C. (2024). Measuring and validating autistic burnout. Autism Research, 17(7), 1417-1449. https://doi.org/10.1002/aur.3129

MedlinePlus. (2025, May 19). Fatigue. U.S. National Library of Medicine. https://medlineplus.gov/ency/article/003088.htm

MedlinePlus. (2026, January 20). Differential diagnosis. U.S. National Library of Medicine. https://medlineplus.gov/lab-tests/differential-diagnosis/

National Institute for Health and Care Excellence. (2022). Depression in adults: Treatment and management (NICE Guideline NG222). https://www.nice.org.uk/guidance/ng222

National Institute of Mental Health. (n.d.). Depression. U.S. Department of Health and Human Services. https://www.nimh.nih.gov/health/publications/depression

National Institute of Mental Health. (n.d.). Mental health medications. U.S. Department of Health and Human Services. https://www.nimh.nih.gov/health/topics/mental-health-medications

Raymaker, D. M., Teo, A. R., Steckler, N. A., Lentz, B., Scharer, M., Delos Santos, A., Kapp, S. K., Hunter, M., Joyce, A., & Nicolaidis, C. (2020). "Having all of your internal resources exhausted beyond measure and being left with no clean-up crew": Defining autistic burnout. Autism in Adulthood, 2(2), 132-143. https://doi.org/10.1089/aut.2019.0079

Substance Abuse and Mental Health Services Administration. (2025, September 26). 988 Suicide & Crisis Lifeline. https://www.samhsa.gov/mental-health/988

World Health Organization. (2019, May 28). Burn-out an "occupational phenomenon": International Classification of Diseases. https://www.who.int/news/item/28-05-2019-burn-out-an-occupational-phenomenon-international-classification-of-diseases

World Health Organization. (2025, August 29). Depressive disorder (depression). https://www.who.int/news-room/fact-sheets/detail/depression

www.ingramcontent.com/pod-product-compliance
Lightning Source LLC
LaVergne TN
LVHW010731061126
851857LV00014B/1426